PEARL'S BOY

A Memoir
by
Marvin Davis Evans

First Printing, June 2010
Published privately by Marvin D. Evans
525 Homestead Lane NE, Apt D 226
Bainbridge Island, WA 98110-2814
mdevans@sounddsl.com

Printed in the United States of America
by Gorham Printing
3718 Mahoney Drive
Centralia, WA 98531
www.gorhamprinting.com

Editor, Cover and Interior Design by:
Kathryn Keve: www.keveoriginals.com

COVER PHOTOGRAPHS
Front Cover
Marvin Evans
Miss Pearl

Back Cover
Our Family – Off to Chicago, 1961
Rev. William Houff & Rev. Marvin D. Evans
    at the 85th Anniversary of University Unitarian Church, Seattle,
Brandywine Under Sail

ISBN 978-0-578-05920-4
Library of Congress Control Number: 2010908586

Evans, Marvin D. Pearl's Boy, A Memoir; includes references to:
1. Lakeside Programming Group, 2. Bill Gates, 3. Kent Evans,
4. Paul Allen, Ric Weiland, Microsoft, 3. The Reverend Robert L. Fulghum.

To Karyn

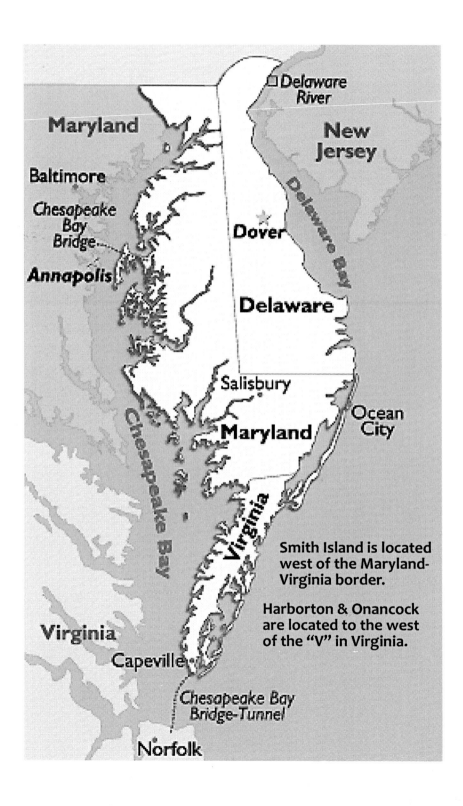

Maryland

Baltimore

Chesapeake
Bay
Bridge

Annapolis

Delaware River

New
Jersey

Delaware Bay

Dover

Delaware

Salisbury

Maryland

Ocean
City

Chesapeake Bay

Virginia

Smith Island is located
west of the Maryland-
Virginia border.

Harborton & Onancock
are located to the west
of the "V" in Virginia.

Virginia

Capeville

Chesapeake Bay
Bridge-Tunnel

Norfolk

Pearl's Boy
Table of Contents

PREFACE

For more than twenty years I have resisted all entreaties to write a memoir. As my 85th birthday looms, the constant and frequent urging from family, dear friends, and even acquaintances motivates me to try my hand.

From my birth in 1925, in Norfolk, Virginia, I have witnessed enormous historical events but more significantly have participated in several social movements and lived a very fulfilling personal life.

Because of several moves my vast collection of files are long gone. Thus I will be relying almost totally on memory. While my memory is still quite good, it is far from perfect, especially with regard to intricate details. Any mistakes found by readers, either of fact or interpretation, are my mistakes, not someone else's.

Sharp minds will likely peruse these pages. If the reaction is Ah! Ha! He left out such and such! the likelihood is you are quite correct. You know about it and I know about it, and now it is best "covered with the mantle of oblivion." That is a quote from one of my foremost literary heroines, Anne Shirley, from the series of eight 20th century novels by Lucy Maud Montgomery. Perhaps you recall this famous literary personality as Anne of Green Gables.

Most people who know me, also know about the untimely loss of our older son. The full text of the Memorial Service for Kent Hood Evans is included as an appendix. This was transcribed from an audio recording and captures his personality much more effectively than anything I could possibly write.

So, here's the story of Pearl's Boy.

(1) WHERE IT ALL BEGAN

If you look at a map of the east coast of the United States, just south of New Jersey, you will see a long peninsula, bounded by the Atlantic Ocean on the east and Chesapeake Bay on the west.

This narrow strip of land is called the Delmarva Peninsula because parts of it are in three states: Delaware, Maryland and Virginia. My family has lived on this peninsula, in both the Maryland and Virginia sections, and on two tiny islands in Chesapeake Bay, for four hundred years. First cousins are still there. My paternal great grandfather, William Evans, was from Smith Island, Maryland, where his family has lived since 1700 and likely longer than that. He moved off the island and settled in the town of Harborton, on the lower Eastern Shore, in the 1850s. My father, Olaus Bowdoin Evans, was born in Harborton in 1886. His mother was descended from Colonel John Wise, whom I understand was on the Eastern Shore prior to 1620.

The two southernmost counties, Accomack and Northampton, both in Virginia, are distinctly rural and have always been that way. U.S. 13, "The Shortest Route from Pines to Palms," runs the length of the peninsula and connects with the Chesapeake Bay Bridge Tunnel to Norfolk and points south. The area is heavily agricultural. There are no large cities, no suburbs and no Interstate highways. The two largest towns on the mainland, Cape Charles at the southernmost tip of the peninsula, and Onancock, have roughly fifteen hundred people each. Chincoteague, on Chincoteague Island, in the Atlantic Ocean, has roughly three times that many people.

Prior to the coming of the automobile, the major means of travel were, first, the New York, Philadelphia and Norfolk (NYP&N) Division of the Pennsylvania Railroad, which operated a railroad down the coast from New York to Cape Charles and a steamboat that crossed Chesapeake Bay from Cape Charles to Norfolk. Secondly, an overnight steamboat came from Baltimore down to Pungoteague Creek (mid-peninsula) with various stops along the way.

I am told by persons competent in the field of genealogy that it is rather unusual for a family to have lived in the same small area of the United States and still be there in 2010. I am certain that I have a huge number of distant relatives still residing in Accomack and Northampton counties. You can easily traverse the entire area, including Smith Island, Maryland and Tangier Island, Virginia in little more than one day, assuming you could engage transportation to the islands.

(2) LIFE IN RURAL VIRGINIA

Beginning when I was fourteen or so, I developed a life-long interest in history and especially the history and culture of that very old and very small county. As I grew into adulthood, I realized that although I was born in the city and am a child of the city (I have never lived in a rural setting), my mother and father parented me in the context of their own upbringing and their experiences of early adulthood.

So, I invite the reader of this memoir to step out of your present-day world and contemplate just a few aspects of life in Harborton, Virginia, from the year 1886, when my father was born, to 1923, when he and my mother moved to Norfolk.

No electricity. No incandescent lights. No running water. No inside plumbing. No electric appliances. No powered heat sources or cooking sources. No daily newspapers. No radio, unless you could afford a battery-powered one.

Owning and feeding a horse, plus a buggy or carriage was beyond the means of most people. The principal means of travel was walking. This explains why the Methodists, the dominant church in the county, tried to have a congregation and a building every three miles. It was quite natural and quite common to live your entire life and not travel more than ten miles from where you were born.

My parents loved each other dearly. My mother had a wonderful sense of humor. When I would inquire how she and my father got together, she would roll her eyes and reply, with a twinkle, "What was I supposed to do?"

It was rare for outsiders to pass through this isolated town, with one important exception. Harborton is located on the south side of Pungoteague Creek and the county road ended at the town wharf. Thus it was not on the way to anywhere. However, and this is a BIG however, the Night Boat to Baltimore docked at Harborton every other night on its round trip to and from Baltimore. Carrying both passengers and freight, it was the main link to the outside world. The steamboat Eastern Shore maintained that route for more than fifty years. Baltimore was much easier to reach than Norfolk. Although the NYP & N railroad ran down the Shore, it was difficult to get from Harborton to the nearest railroad station, and after you reached Cape Charles you had to take a steamboat to Norfolk.

Socially there was a pervasive sense of isolation and what can only be described as fundamentalism. I am not suggesting that every resident was a believing Christian or an active church member. I am suggesting, however, that what historians describe as "Primitive Methodism" was dominant and in many ways the controlling religious and social force in the town. Even in my childhood, in the 1930s, the Harborton Methodist Episcopal Church, South was the core and center of religious and social life. Unless your finances were such that you could afford passage on the Eastern Shore, and had some reason or necessity to go to Baltimore, or unless you were what they call a waterman and made your living on the water there was a good probability that you would be born, live and die without leaving the Town of Harborton.

The summer days spent there during my early childhood were delightful. There were several general stores of various sizes and, praised be, the Sears & Roebuck and Montgomery Ward catalogs.

Soon after my great grandfather, William Evans (George's son) moved to Harborton in the 1850s, my grandfather, Egbert G. Evans, was born in 1858. "Captain Eg" apparently did quite well for himself. He went to sea and at some point obtained a license as a Master from the United States Coast Guard. This was no small achievement. Such licenses, as either a Deck Officer or an Engine Room Officer were difficult to attain and required years of study, examinations and time on duty. A friend of mine who has a license as a physician and as a Master says without hesitation that the latter was much more difficult to attain.

My understanding is that during early adulthood, my grandfather Captain Eg owned and operated sailing schooners and transported cargo along the Atlantic Coast, as far north as Halifax and Lunenburg in Nova Scotia, and as far south as Savannah, Georgia. It seems he did quite well because Evans House, a very nice home on the east side of the county road, was built in 1884 and still stands.

Egbert G. Evans married Mary Susan Wise and on April 8, 1886, my father, Olaus Bowdoin Evans, was born in Harborton. Family tradition portrays what might be called a "Marriage of Circumstance" since the well-nigh universal assumption in that day and age was that men and women would get married, usually at quite a young age. Bachelors and Old Maids were regarded with suspicion, ridiculed, with no small measure of derision. Even worse, they were not fulfilling their God-given mission and purpose in life, which was to reproduce and populate the earth.

Good manners probably dictate that I should be more compassionate yet the reality is that Mary Wise Evans was a "pill." She was cold, demanding, inflexible, opinionated – a fundamentalist True Believer. It would be safe to conclude that she was a Child of Her Environment and she never had any opportunity whatsoever to grow beyond the myopia of her birthplace.

Captain Eg and Miss Mary had a number of children yet only one additional child survived to adulthood. Marvin Keener Evans was born on March 31, 1889.

He is the uncle for whom I was named. Interestingly, Miss Mary named him for two bishops of the Methodist Church: Enoch Mather Marvin and John Christian Keener. Fortunately, my mother didn't fancy the name "Keener," so she gave me the middle name "Davis," a name used frequently in her family.

At this point the story takes a tragic turn, one that had a lasting effect on future events.

My uncle Marvin "followed the water." That was the term for anyone who took a job, any job, on a boat. In May of 1910 he was on a trial run of the tugboat Cape Charles, being built in Camden, New

Jersey, for the Pennsylvania Railroad. The railroad had its own fleet of barges and tugs and routinely transported railroad freight cars across Chesapeake Bay from Cape Charles to Norfolk. The tug had a triple compound, coal-fired steam engine. A fitting failed and Marvin was scalded. His parents rushed to the hospital in Camden to be at his bedside. The newspapers reported on the matter almost daily. He was critically ill. He showed some improvement. He might recover. No, he was worse.

Meanwhile, Captain Eg was taken ill. Father and son died in the same hospital within thirty minutes of each other. They are buried in the churchyard at St. George's Episcopal Church in Pungoteague. The newspaper in Camden reported that at the time of Marvin's death, O.B. was at sea, and had been notified of the death of his father and his brother.

Miss Mary lived another twenty-two years but never really recovered from that terrible tragedy. She lived at Evans House until she died in 1932 yet life was never the same again. She became more rigid and inflexible. Evans House was easily made comfortable for two families and she and a widowed sister, Ella Boggs Agathoin, always known as "Boggie," lived there together. A third sister, Rose Wise Mears, also a widow, lived just across a lane that separated the two houses. Boggie and Rose had various children and thus there was a large extended family.

Rose had a son, A. Quinton Mears, who was one of my childhood "heroes" – of a sort. "A.Q." went off to New York to become a stock broker. Just before the Crash of 1929, he cashed out and returned to Harborton to live with his mother. He bought back in at pennies on the dollar and never worked another day. He filled the house with antiques and expensive carpets, grew blue ribbon roses, had a beautiful Packard Motor car, read the Wall Street Journal and lived the quiet, well-ordered life of a country gentleman. Even when working in the garden he was impeccably dressed. Much to the consternation of the family, I adored him.

The death of Marvin left Miss Mary with only one living offspring, my father. I know relatively little about the first thirty-seven years of his life. I know he left the private Pungoteague Academy at a fairly young age and went to sea. He must have had a relatively good educational grounding because he obtained his license as a Chief Engineer in the Merchant Marine.

On December 10, 1912, O.B. married my mother, Pearl Ruth Hutchinson, at the Craddockville Methodist Church in Craddockville, Virginia.

Pearl Hutchinson was one of the six children, three boys and three girls, born to Benjamin Davis Hutchinson and Emma Sturgis Hutchinson, on a small farm at Davis Wharf, Virginia, a small village on Occahannock Creek, which is south of Pungoteague Creek. Davis Wharf was a much smaller community than Harborton. It was a regular stop for the Eastern Shore, thus it had a wharf and shed, a general store and post office, and houses along the main county road which ended at the wharf. Rich farm land surrounded the town and produce such as potatoes, a major crop, could be barreled and shipped to Baltimore.

I know relatively little about my parents until they moved to Norfolk in 1923. They had a daughter, Roberta, who died in the flu epidemic that occurred after the First World War, and a daughter, Christine, born in 1919 and still living in 2009, although with an advanced case of Alzheimer's Disease.

One account has it that O.B. and a brother-in-law, B. Clyde Hutchinson, "kept store" in Craddockville for several years. I have no documentation of that.

(3) GROWING UP IN THE DARK AGES

The Chief, age 37, Pearl, almost 32, and Christine, age 4, moved to Norfolk in the fall of 1923. My mother was the only one of the six siblings who left Accomack County during their working years.

My father had obtained a job as an engineer on the steam tug Wellfleet. The company owned another tug, the P.F. Martin, and our family thought of that as the name of the company.

The Wellfleet was a no-nonsense vessel, perhaps built in the 1880s, with a triple compound steam engine and a coal-fired boiler.

While looking for a place to live, our family stayed at a rooming-boarding house operated by Mrs. C.C. Sivills and her husband. My recollection is that it was on Claiborne Avenue in the Brambleton section of Norfolk. This street was an entry-point to the Norfolk Shipbuilding and Dry Dock Company, the port-of-call for the Martin fleet.

My parents soon rented a modest frame house at 1730 Claiborne Avenue, the house in which I was born on December 2, 1925.

Like so many neighborhoods of that era, Brambleton was mixed, with a diverse population socially and economically, yet all white. Neighborhoods were much more diverse than they are in 2009. I spent my entire growing up years in diverse neighborhoods and diverse schools.

One of Brambleton's chief claims to fame was that it was in the lee of the coal-fired Reeves Avenue Generating Plant, owned by the

Virginia Electric and Power Company, known as VEPCO. This was very much like living in South Side Chicago when the steel mills were operating at full capacity. My mother talked about changing my clothes three and four times a day.

Members of my family, on both my father's and my mother's side, have been active members of the Methodist Church for at least ten generations including my generation and three that follow after me. In fact, members of the family still belong to the Craddockville United Methodist Church.

Located in the same block with our house was the McKendree Methodist Church. This church quickly became the center of our religious and social life.

Memories of my early childhood are not particularly clear or compelling. My father was often away from home yet my mother was quite outgoing and we had a large circle of friendly neighbors – men, women and children all ages.

It was during elementary school and beyond that I had illnesses that affect my life to this day. I truly wish I knew more about this. I had severe sinus and ear ailments, frequently having to have one or both ears lanced without adequate anesthesia. I had hay fever. Some illnesses or perhaps genetics left me with an almost non-existent muscle structure. My arms and legs have remained quite thin. And I must have had rheumatic fever of something of the sort, which means that for more than seventy years I have had severe pain and limited movement in my arms and legs. I was confined to bed for weeks at a time. I am 6'4" and weighed 152 pounds until my early forties.

It was during this period of continuing, protracted illness that the very special bond between my mother and me was formed. Without her constant care and loving encouragement I might well not have survived. She watched over me night and day, without complaining or feeling sorry for herself. We shared this experience at a very deep level. My sister, Christine, was seven years older. She has stated, with considerable validity, that I was an only child.

Our household was virtually bookless and I developed a fascination with newspapers at a very early age. I was reading when I entered kindergarten in the fall of 1930. This fascination with newspapers has had an enormous impact on my life. I have never lived in New York City yet have subscribed to *The New York Times* for forty-two years.

My family owned a 1926 Ford Model T Touring Car that was hand-cranked. My mother was the principal driver because engine room personnel on tugs and ships never have to pay any attention to where they are going or what other traffic happens to be nearby. The wheel house folks do that. I don't recall ever riding in the car with my father driving.

I still have great affection for the Sunday afternoon drives that were so characteristic of that time. We would frequently drive out to the surrounding countryside of Princess Anne County, with lots of truck farming done largely by Dunkards, a splinter group from the German Baptist Bretherens, similar to the Mennonites. Or, we would take the lovely drive out Hampton Boulevard to the Naval Operating Base (N.O.B.) where the public could actually go aboard those marvelous battleships and aircraft carriers. The galley personnel were always Filipino and I can smell the cooking to this day. Perhaps we would stop for a five cent cone at Hundley's, a small, independent ice cream store with the best lemon custard ice cream I ever tasted, before or since.

About this time, at age six or seven, I began to get an inkling of the most formative aspects of my life. First, my parents had a truly co-equal marriage and I thought that was how it was supposed to be. I learned much later, to my distress, that many, if not most, marriages were anything but co-equal, certainly not in the 1930s, or even later in this country and today in much of the world. Secondly, I learned that my parents truly loved, respected and cherished each other, and I thought that was how it was supposed to be. Thirdly, I learned that they really and truly loved me, and again I thought this was how it was supposed to be. I doubt that any child in all of human history has ever had parents who loved him or her more than my parents loved me.

This is also the period during which my lifetime interest in government and politics began to develop. My parents bought a floor model radio. It was basically a piece of furniture, a cabinet with legs. The tuner and amplifier, quite large in those days, were mounted near the top and the speaker or speakers were located near the bottom, with a tiny dial. Living a rather circumscribed life, it immediately became my window on the world. I followed the 1932 presidential election with keen interest, even though I was not quite seven years of age.

Radio became my constant companion. I listened to news, to the fifteen minute serials of which there were many, to the many popular network programs and especially to the wonderful Big Band broadcasts from famous public ballrooms in New York, Chicago, San Francisco and many other cities.

My first major purchase was a small table model radio. My mother persuaded a furniture store – Charles and Leroy Ford, "The Boys You Know," to let me have it while I made weekly payments. Every Saturday I went downtown and paid fifty cents until the $9.95 was paid off.

I could secret the small set under the bed covers with me in my unheated bedroom and listen far into the night. It was a tremendous diversion during my long periods of illness. It enriched the life of a blue collar kid from the wrong side of the tracks.

While on her annual "state visit" in 1932, an event much-dreaded by Christine and me, Grandmother Evans had a heart attack and died instantly. Her body was embalmed and taken back to Harborton where there was a viewing in her living room at Evans House. It was the first time I had seen an embalmed body and I can still recall the image as though the event happened yesterday.

My father was the only heir and it is possible that he received a small inheritance. In any event my parents purchased a modest, almost new house at 2801 Marlboro Avenue, in the Chesterfield Heights section of Norfolk.

Although on the wrong side of the tracks, as was Brambleton, "Chickenfeed Heights," as we called it, was a good place in which to start my life.

The area was even more diverse than Brambleton. It had everything from dilapidated four room cottages to very large houses on Chesterfield Boulevard, which ran along the banks of the Elizabeth

River. There were no retail stores, professional offices or businesses of any kind. There were only two or three duplex apartment buildings and no larger ones. It was almost entirely single family, although some households were doubled-up, a common practice in that day and age. One had to walk about half a mile to a community called Riverside to find two small grocery stores, a drug store, a tavern, a barber shop and a small shipyard for the repair and maintenance of commercial vessels.

Our house, which was relatively new, had been constructed by Jesse Parker, a small-scale building contractor, as a home for himself and his wife. If I remember correctly, the house was situated on a corner lot on the southeast corner of Marlboro Avenue and Norchester Avenue.

It was frame with a red tile roof. It had a large porch and front entry directly into the living room. The first floor also had my parent's bedroom, a living room, a dining room, a small hallway with steps leading upstairs and down to the basement, one small bathroom with a tub only, a kitchen, a pantry and small back porch with a back door. Upstairs was one large bedroom and a very small room which the Parker's had designed as his wife's sewing room. The house also had a very attractive side entrance with steps going down to a full daylight basement and steps going up to the main floor. It was small for a family of four but adequate for our needs. My mother lived there more than twenty-five years.

I recall only two churches although perhaps there were others. There was a small Christadelphian Church and the Chesterfield Heights Methodist Church. Although situated in the city, it had many characteristics of a rural church. When we first moved to the neighborhood, the Methodist Church was a very small frame building with one large multi-purpose room and a few classrooms but little else. There was a parsonage for the minister several blocks away. Later a more substantial sanctuary was built.

We continued to attend the McKendree Church until at some point our car was stolen and stripped. After that we never owned a car and I did not acquire one until 1951.

Since it was no longer convenient to attend McKendree we began attending the church in Chesterfield Heights. This small Methodist congregation was the central focus of our religious and social life for my parents and me. I simply cannot overemphasize this fact. We had no car, there were no amusements of any kind in the neighborhood, we had very little money, and we were devout and devoted Methodists. My parents had grown up in that motif and so did I.

When we moved to Chesterfield Heights I entered the neighborhood school in grade two or three. The small brick building, stout with few amenities, was located on the northeastern edge of the community yet within manageable distance either on foot or on my ever-present bicycle.

One of the truly defining characteristics of my life is that I have always been a good student, and a well-dressed, polite, courteous respectful one at that. Thus I was always in the top group academically and socially. This reality has had an enormous effect on my life. I am blessed with a quick mind. I enjoy being asked to do things. I enjoy doing what I am asked to do and try to do it well. That's my temperament.

The nation was in the throes of the Great Depression yet somehow the neighborhood was quite stable. I went through ten years of public school with the same group of friends and we were basically all in the same situation. And, most significantly, our "pack" consisted of both boys and girls.

The group included Mildred McWilliams – literally the girl next door. She, and to a much lesser extent her younger sister, Dorothy (Dottie) became a devoted friend. It was from her, and with her, that I learned to have friendships with girls and women without even a hint of romance. To this day, I enjoy significant friendships with girls and women of all ages.

This experience has broadened my outlook and deepened my enjoyment of life so that I know how to relate meaningfully with men and women. I have also been influenced greatly in this regard by Deborah Tannen, the Georgetown University linguist and author of several important books, including *You Just Don't Understand: Women and Men in Conversation* and *The Argument Culture*.

Even at an early age my mother trusted me to behave myself, be reasonably careful, not do anything rash, and stay out of trouble. I was given what I like to call freedom of the city quite early on. I was permitted to go pretty much where I wanted to go.

When we first moved to Chesterfield Heights, the neighborhood was served by a streetcar line. The line dead-ended just two blocks from our house. I could sit on the window seat in the dining room, watch the car go east on the next street (Kimball Terrace), wait for the motorman to flip the seats and the trolley, and then catch the car as it headed back downtown. We had a Shopper's Pass, valid during off hours, during weekdays and all day on Saturday and Sunday.

Later, the streetcar line was replaced with buses which went through the neighborhood but not on a route that retraced its steps.

Childhood activities were simple, inexpensive and fun. By pre-adolescence, winter was filled with roller skating, bicycle riding, toy electric train sets, playing card games, board games, fudge-making, taffy pulls, marbles, mumble-the-peg, rock-scissors-paper and anything else we could come up with.

In the summers we continued with many of these same activities plus one enormously important attraction, namely the Elizabeth River, which was perhaps a hundred yards from our back door. This is where I became the wharf rat that I continue to be. Our section of the river was one or two miles long, between the Campostella Bridge on one end and the Virginian Railway bridge on the other end. The river at that point had very little traffic except occasionally a vessel would go to a Ford Motor Company assembly plant located just before the railway bridge, on the far side of the river.

This river was the main focus of my life. We caught hard crabs, gathered soft crabs, and swam—often using the raw sewage outflow pipe as a diving platform. Most of all, we sailed. We couldn't afford even a rudimentary rowboat so The Chief (my father) and I built a simple sailing kayak. We used barrel stays, canvas and wood and improvised a mast, lee boards, a bow sprit, and two sails. We also built a cart so we could get the kayak from the house to the river.

I spent hours, days, weeks sailing that kayak. Several friends had them and we went on overnight camping trips farther up the river, beyond the railroad bridge. That's where and when and how I developed a lifetime love for sailing.

"Time in the country" was a popular prescription in those days, for both children and adults, and thus I often went to stay with relatives in Accomack County. A commercial company, I think it was the Virginia Ferry Corporation, operated a modern vehicle-passenger ferry service across Chesapeake Bay. Using several modes of transportation I could make my way across Chesapeake Bay to lower Northampton County. At this point an antiquated bus, operated by the Eastern Shore Transit Company, would deposit me at the small roadside Sinclair gas station operated by my aunt and uncle, Mary and Richard Nottingham, on the west side of U.S. 13, midway between the towns of Melfa and Onley. The structure, built by Uncle Richard with his own hands, was quite close to the highway. There were two gravity-flow gas pumps. There was a tiny store in the front of the building with pop, candy, cigarettes, cheese cut to order and more, with family living quarters in the back.

I loved it! I absolutely loved it. I pumped gas and waited on customers and stocked the old-fashioned pop case, and swept the floor and picked up outside and did whatever I was asked to do. It was heaven for a young boy and gave me my first real experience serving the public.

Fortunately I was one of these youngsters who could entertain himself. I still wasn't reading books but loved magazines, especially Life, and newspapers and the huge mail order catalogs. Sears and Montgomery Ward were the WalMarts of their day and age.

After I had stayed a spell there, my Aunt Mary would fire up the trusted Plymouth and drive me to another relative's home, usually my mother's youngest brother, Leonard Hutchinson, and his wife Elizabeth, in the village of Craddockville.

Frequently my mother would also come and the two of us would make a much wider circuit among her three brothers and two sisters, and their families. This enabled me to wander around in Harborton and Pungoteague and listen to the old-timers who seemed to spend their waking hours visiting together on wooden benches and chairs at the various general stores.

Visitors, strangers, and outsiders were few and far between in the town and villages. I was tall and thin and quite noticeable. It seems that everywhere I went the question was always, "Who's that?" Invariably, the response was, "Oh, that's Pearl's Boy." Not Marvin Evans, not Pearl Evans' boy. Just Pearl's Boy.

In more ways than I can count, I am Pearl's Boy to this day.

Some summers, when my mother came, Aunt Mary would take us by car to visit family friends who lived in Ocean View, Delaware. Our family traveled very little indeed so this was a great adventure. We visited Rehoboth Beach, Bethany Beach, Fenwick Island, and other places in that area.

The husband and father of this family, a tall, thin, nervous man named Nelson Dolby, was the steward on the tug Eureka, also owned by the Martin Company, and also based in Norfolk. A favorite excursion of my childhood was to be invited to go aboard from Norfolk to Newport News to "coal-up" – to replenish the huge quantity of coal required as fuel for these seagoing tugs. We would take along ukeleles, sing until we were hoarse, eat vast quantities of what seemed like the best food on the planet, and generally have a great time.

* * *

In Norfolk, the Methodist Church continued to be the focus of our religious and social life.

We simply showed up whenever there was an activity appropriate for our age, and sometimes even when it wasn't. By the time I was about twelve, the "blood and thunder" Bible stories didn't appeal to me, and I couldn't stand the adult male teacher, so I angled an appointment as secretary and treasurer of the Sunday School, with a friendly adult actually maintaining the bank account and paying the bills. I had my own desk and kept the attendance records, counted the offering, and thought of myself as being quite important and useful. That's how I learned that being secretary or treasurer or a combination of the two is absolutely the best job.

I learned to speak in public, mainly in school and at church, before both adults and young people, how to usher, and even how to pray spontaneously in public without any advance notice. I also formed the notion, with me to this day, that church is a very special place and deserves to be taken seriously. I was never forced or compelled to go to Sunday School or to the church service, yet there was a silent assumption that if I didn't feel like going then I certainly wouldn't feel like doing anything else "strenuous" the rest of the day, such as going off with friends.

The most important transition, by far, came when I graduated from the Chesterfield Heights Elementary School in the spring of 1937, just short of twelve years of age and that fall, entered William Henry Ruffner Junior High School, where I was to spend the next three years of my life.

Ruffner was a large school, grades seven, eight and nine, located at least two miles from my home and situated on the edge of the downtown area just a short distance from the main railroad station. Barely on the other side of the tracks, I commuted on public transportation.

To say that the transition was difficult and intimidating is an understatement. From my perspective the school was simply huge. The day began in homeroom and we changed classes every period. The teachers were almost all women, either unmarried or widowed, and some were formidable taskmasters.

My sister, Christine, was a good student and my parents expected no less of me. She was remembered quite well. The expectation was that as her younger brother, I too, would be a good student. I decided to surpass her as a student, and that is what I set out to do. Then I realized that the same expectation would prevail when I reached Maury High School, so I decided to hop on that train and ride it as far as it would take me. That turned out to be a very wise decision indeed.

As it turned out, on balance Ruffner was a good experience. I mastered the very different course load and schedule, learned to organize my work, and use my time wisely. I came to understand at an even deeper level that if you did what the teachers asked you to do, did it on time, and did it well, your position in the scheme of things was secured. You earned the reputation of being a serious student. I rode that "train" for six years of public school, four years of college, and two years of theological school and it served me well.

* * *

During this period, the family situation changed in very important ways. My memory of this period is quite vague and Christine no longer has any memory, so this is what I recall.

At some point, my father was no longer employed on the tug Well-fleet. He secured a job as an engineer with the Wood Towing Corporation, a large towing company operating out of a small office on Roanoke Dock, in downtown Norfolk with a repair and maintenance yard in Brambleton. The Wood fleet operated primarily in the Port of Hampton Roads (Norfolk, Portsmouth, Newport News, etc) and the vast Chesapeake Bay and its many tributaries, such as the James, the York and the Potomac Rivers. They also handled ships docking and undocking in Norfolk Harbor.

The Chief's first job was on The Bay and its tributaries and several times he took me with him for several days or a week or more. His private cabin on the Nonpareil, adjacent to the engine room, must have had two bunks. In any event, these trips were a wonderful adventure for a young teenage boy. I had absolutely no interest in compound steam engines and spent every possible moment in the Pilot House, which they called the Wheel House. The helmsmen weren't all that enamored with steering so I was permitted to steer the tug for hours on end, usually with four, five or six barges strung out behind on hawsers. The Bay is quite shallow so the course was frequently buoy to buoy. Excellent experience and training for someone who twenty-five years later began to sail the waters of western Washington and southwest British Columbia.

The Chief was diagnosed with Type 2 adult-onset diabetes. He was on injected insulin the rest of his life and his general health declined gradually, although he lived another twelve years or so. My mother, understandably, gave him her primary attention and much of the family routine was influenced by his situation and his needs.

Meanwhile Christine graduated from high school, took a rigorous course at Kee's Secretarial College, and secured employment as a legal secretary. She continued to live at home but was quite busy with her job and various boyfriends.

My opportunities for what might be called "special" activities were few and far between. There was no money for summer camp, dancing lessons, travel, or even a small day sailer. Two friends owned a one-design called a Moth, and I was able to use it occasionally.

Even so, we were able to do many things, such as go to the movies or go bowling downtown or take jaunts to Virginia Beach. One friend had a very nice phonograph and we spent many hours listening to music on 78 rpm records, and dancing after a fashion. We spent a huge amount of time playing board games, especially Monopoly.

At age fourteen or so, an interest in girls surfaced and I have enjoyed their company ever since. During the ninth grade I began to have dates with girls, most of them very nice. I liked their company and the experience contributed greatly to the enjoyment of my teen years and to my growth as a person. I could write much about this yet my memories of this time are too vague and untrustworthy.

Entering Matthew Fontaine Maury High School, in the fall of 1940, was a significant event but much less stressful than going to Ruffner.

Maury was a large school with perhaps fifteen hundred students and was still farther from home. If I didn't happen to catch the transit bus that went directly to the school, I had to transfer downtown.

Norfolk in those days was a city of about 130,000 people, a major seaport and heavily dominated by the United States Armed Forces. It had a huge Naval Operating Base, a Naval Air Station, a large Navy Yard, Fort Story and many other military installations. It was rigidly segregated by race − white and colored. The black population had their own city within a city, dominated by Church Street, their main thoroughfare. There was also a sizeable Asian population.

There were two high schools for white students: Maury, the blue collar school, and Granby High School, the white collar school. I was most fortunate to live on the wrong side of the tracks and go to Maury because that is where I most definitely belonged.

Maury was a truly excellent experience for me. I came alive in ways that set the course of my life to this day. This requires some explanation.

While I was growing up, and even much later, Virginia was what I would call a very backward-looking place. They idealized the society they had before the Civil War or the War Between the States or the War for Southern Independence. They longed for an "Idealized Past" that in reality never existed. The Virginia State Song, designated as such by the General Assembly in 1940 was an outrageous ode to a past better forgotten entitled Carry Me Back to Old Virginny. Here's the first verse:

Carry me back to old Virginny,
There's where the cotton and the corn and 'tatoes grow,
There's where the birds warble sweet in the springtime.
That's where the old darkey's heart am longed to go,
There's where I labored so hard for old massa,
Day after day in the field of yellow corn,
No place on earth do I love more sincerely,
Than old Virginny, the state where I was born.

In addition, there was much religious hatred, prejudice, discrimination and just plain meanness. Catholics and Jews were discriminated against in various ways, some subtle and some not so subtle. The same was true for Asians and foreigners in general.

There was also hatred of anything and everything that was identified as Northern – Abraham Lincoln, Franklin Roosevelt, Eleanor Roosevelt, the Yankees, the Battle Hymn of the Republic, and so on. The list seemed to be endless.

I had friends, schoolmates, and acquaintances in many of these categories and all of them seemed like quite normal human beings to me. Yet because of family upbringing and social pressure I held to the old ways. This in effect tore me apart mentally and emotionally and spiritually and led to an inner turmoil that lasted about a dozen years.

With a significance and importance that I cannot describe adequately, my history teacher during my sophomore year, 1940-41, gave me a lasting image of the way out of my dilemma. Her name was Annie Belle Crowder and if I remember correctly she was from rural North Carolina. Much of who I am today can be traced back to her.

Miss Crowder impressed on me what she truly believed – these words from the Declaration of Independence.

> "We hold these truths to be self-evident, that all men (persons) are created equal, that they are endowed by their Creator with certain unalienable rights, that among these are Life, Liberty and the pursuit of Happiness."

After I had completed the courses she taught, we became friends. She frequently stayed in her classroom after the school day ended. I would drop by and we would talk about what I would now describe as the Second Principle of Unitarian Universalists, namely "Justice, equity and compassion in human relations."

She thought I was too heavily involved with a girl with whom she thought I had little in common (she was correct) and guided me through that maze.

In retrospect, she started me on my life long journey of "Living in The Transforming Present" and I am deeply indebted to her.

Another important lesson I learned at Maury, and even at Ruffner, was attention to detail. I had teachers: Virginia H. Johnson for English; Rachel Taylor and Laura Ogden Williams for math; Frances Hardy for physics; Roberta Day Hodgkin for geography; Kate Gillette for chemistry, and a host of others whose names I have forgotten, who insisted relentlessly and without fear or favor that we get it right, including and especially the small stuff. This ranks as one of the most valuable and useful lessons I have ever learned.

Life at Maury and at home moved along. Then, an event occurred that changed my life forever. There have been several such events in my life and I wonder to this day whether they were pure happenstance.

(4) A DIFFERENT WORLD: COLLEGE and WORLD WAR II

I turned seventeen on December 2, 1942, mid-way through my senior year in high school. I knew I would have another year before I became eligible for Selective Service. My mind was set on going to college. I was accepted for an accelerated program at what was then Virginia Polytechnic Institute (VPI) beginning in January of 1943 but the program was cancelled for lack of interest. They neglected to tell me it had been cancelled and I actually packed a trunk and took the train to Blacksburg, only to have to return to Maury and ask to be readmitted.

I had gone to summer school the previous summer and had a very light course load so I worked as a volunteer in the Assistant Principal's Office and also as a soda jerk at Tatem's Drug Store in Brambleton.

I still had to take the much-hated farce called "Physical Education," which wasn't very physical and certainly wasn't education. One day I was in the boy's locker room, in my birthday suit when a well-dressed gentleman stuck his head in the door and asked, "Is Marvin Evans here?"

"Yes," I replied.

"I would like to speak with you briefly when you finish dressing."

I came out. He introduced himself and without any interview or further conversation, he offered me a scholarship to Randolph-Macon College.

I knew about the college although I had never seen the campus. It was, and still is, a small, excellent liberal arts college, loosely affiliated with the Methodist Church, and located in Ashland, Virginia, a small town sixteen miles north of Richmond, on U.S. 1.

Until the 1970s the college was for men, there being a sister school, Randolph-Macon Women's College, in Lynchburg.

Because World War II was at its height and the United States was running out of manpower, the college had very few students. They were struggling to stay open. They had restricted endowment funds available for scholarships so they sent a member of the staff of the Athletic Department on a tour of high schools throughout the state, looking for available young men or what I would call "live bodies." Everyone in 1943 was looking for live bodies.

I accepted without even consulting my parents.

They wanted students immediately if not sooner. Methodists have long understood that Money Is Money. So, two days after graduation I took the train to Ashland and enrolled at Randolph-Macon.

The school, founded in 1830, had always struggled financially and the combination of the Great Depression and World War II had almost been its undoing. The buildings and other facilities had seen better days, and they did not even operate a dining room. Students made their own arrangements to eat at one of the several boarding houses close to the campus.

Other than time spent with relatives, described earlier, I had never really been away from home.

One saving grace was that the Walter Hines Page Library was in the center of the campus, just a few yards from the dormitory. A whole new world – a world I had never explored – the world in which I live to this day – opened up before me. I began my lifelong love affair with books.

The student body was not very large. It was mainly pre-medical students, pre-ministerial students and young men who had not entered the armed forces. Courses offered were largely those needed for graduation by advanced students. For example, introductory German was Scientific German, which is complicated and presumes a working knowledge of the language.

The Methodist Church that served the small town was on the campus and I made friends with residents of the town. Because the student body was small, there was much informal social contact with faculty and staff.

We all had freshman beanies in the school colors, lemon and black, so you could walk to the traffic light on U.S. 1, a main highway from Maine to Florida, and a townsperson would delightedly take you into Richmond, a bustling capital city with great amenities, including GIRLS, at Westhampton College of the University of Richmond, or the Richmond Professional Institute (RPI), now Virginia Commonwealth University. On the north end of the city there was a huge truck stop where Ashland residents always kept an eye open for the lemon and black beanies.

Or, you could raise your thumb in a northerly direction and go to the beautiful campus of Mary Washington College in Fredericksburg. which was predominately women, if not completely so.

Very shortly after I arrived in Ashland, the U.S. Army brought in an Army Specialized Training Unit, known by the acronym ASTP.

> Take down that Service Flag, mother,
> Your son's in ASTP.
> He'll never be wounded in action,
> Finding the square root of three.

The college emptied the dormitories in order to house the soldiers and I joined a social fraternity that had a large house with a dining room. It was largely an arrangement of mutual convenience and benefit. They wanted to keep the house occupied and operating and I needed a place to live and eat. Yet I really didn't belong there.

I turned 18 on December 2, 1943, and registered for Selective Service. My mother was convinced that I would fail the physical examination and be classified 4F, yet the army was desperate and I went through with flying colors, even though I had poor vision and poor hearing.

Rather than wait to be summoned, I volunteered for induction. The necessary procedures gave me time to complete the fall semester and I was inducted into the army at Fort George G. Meade, Maryland, on February 26, 1944.

I am not inclined to write at length about my army service. I was a communications specialist in Company B of the 89th Chemical Mortar Company, which was equipped with a 4.2" rifled barrel heavy mortar. We trained in Colorado and Oklahoma and went to England in December of 1944. We spent two months there gathering our equipment, and then participated in the final push to liberate western Europe in the late winter and early spring of 1945. We saw some combat service but suffered very few casualties. We arrived back in the United States on July 4, 1945, headed to Japan, and were stationed at Fort Jackson, South Carolina, when World War II ended.

The actual invasion of Japan would have been a dangerous venture for a heavy mortar company and I have never really come to terms with the bombing of Hiroshima and Nagasaki. Had I been in President Truman's shoes, I think I would have done what he did. I am still convinced that actual combat, kill or be killed, is a nontransferable experience and cannot be understood until and unless you have been there. No one I have ever talked with who hasn't been in combat even begins to understand that experience.

There was a gradual mustering out of the men and women in the armed forces and I was discharged at Fort Sam Houston, Texas, on April 12, 1946.

While stationed at Fort Jackson, South Carolina, near Columbia, I developed a significant relationship with a lovely young woman who lived there and was a brilliant student at the University of South Carolina.

I was sorely tempted to transfer and become a "Gamecock," but South Carolina was much more in the Dark Ages than Virginia, so I returned to Randolph-Macon. This may have been a mistake. One never knows about such things. I have long since lost contact with the young woman and for all these years have wondered what happened to her. She was smart, attractive, and a truly wonderful person.

Back I went to the "oaks and maples" of Ashland. With the advent of the G.I. Bill the college expanded quite rapidly to about four hundred students.

For 116 years Randolph-Macon had taken very young boys, often sixteen or so, from the hamlets and farms, towns and cities of Virginia, and made men of them. Now they were faced with hundreds of veterans who had won a war, many of them older than most previous graduates, many who were married with children, and many who had attained high ranks and commanded units far larger than the student body and faculty and staff combined.

I was a good example. During my final months, I served as Battalion Sergeant Major, the ranking non-commissioned officer in an army unit of 605 soldiers.

They simply didn't know what to do with us, nor could they have been expected to know. A Great Revolution in American life was taking place in their very midst. Nothing like it had ever happened in the history of the world. No nation had ever sent millions of its finest young men to college at public expense. Veterans went and their sisters and female cousins insisted on going too. Transformation was everywhere.

My congenital eye defect caught up with me and steered me away from physics, my great love, and I declared a major in history and a minor in government.

The fraternity house simply didn't work for me and through my friendship with the person in charge of student housing I was able to secure one of the very few single rooms on the entire campus.

Then I experienced another life-changing transformation. Obviously I was required to take a full load of courses, accumulate hours and quality credits, and I did that quite successfully. Yet the spoon-feeding that dominates public education to this day just didn't work for me. So I set out to learn how to self-educate.

The first few weeks of the semester I would master the text book, read any other required books, and write the usual term paper. Having accomplished that, I was then free to really study the subject and venture wherever my curiosity and my interests took me. This was a fascinating experience.

I also had ample opportunity to participate in a wide variety of campus organizations and activities, and develop my leadership skills. This was one of the truly formative periods of my young adulthood and I absolutely loved it. I developed and strengthened the talents and habits that still enrich my life beyond description. I became what I would describe as a self-starter. I was frequently in trouble with the powers that be because attending classes wasn't all that exciting or appealing. My wealthy Uncle Sam paid my tuition. If I purchase season tickets to something, that doesn't mean I have to attend every performance or event.

Dating was also a major activity. I often say that I majored in girls and minored in history and government. I met a lovely young woman, now deceased, and we went together for more than five years.

During these years the college did a major revision of the curriculum and, among other things instituted a senior project as a degree requirement. I was exempt from this requirement because I had enrolled in 1943. However, the professors in the History Department were interested in a pilot project or a trial run so I agreed to see what I could do.

Three days a week I commuted to the Virginia State Library in Richmond (where I subsequently worked for 11 years) and did a major research paper entitled "The Richmond Press On The Eve Of The Civil War." This was a study of the editorial content of the five major newspapers published in Richmond during the twelve months preceding the outbreak of hostilities in 1861. The paper was published in 1951 in The John P. Branch Historical Papers of Randolph-Macon College.

I graduated in 1949, with membership in Phi Beta Kappa (scholarship) and Omicron Delta Kappa (leadership.)

Randolph-Macon was definitely the right place for me. I received an excellent education from an outstanding faculty, I learned how to educate myself, and I grew and matured as a person.

(5) WILL THERE BE ANY GIRLS LEFT FOR ME?

When I graduated from Randolph-Macon College (R-M), with a B.A. degree in history, I still had benefits remaining under the G.I. Bill of Rights. My major professor, William Alexander Mabry, strongly urged me to go to Graduate School at Duke University in Durham, North Carolina. I also had a friend and classmate, George Oliver, who had completed his work at R-M early and was a student there.

I took the Graduate Record Exam, was admitted at Duke, and arrived there in the fall of 1949. George Oliver and I shared a double room in the graduate quadrangle.

To put the matter simply, I was not right for them, they were not right for me, I was tired of studying, I ran out of money, and I wasn't interested in staying there.

Then, happenstance intervened again. My major professor at Duke, Charles S. Sydnor, received a routine circular from the Archives Division of the Virginia State Library, in Richmond. They were expanding their staff and had several vacancies at the entry level, which they described as Archivist A. I applied for one of the vacancies, was hired and stayed there eleven years.

I moved to Richmond, rented a room in a rooming house on West Grace Street in the Fan District, and began my first real salaried job.

The Virginia State Library (VSL) shared space with the State Supreme Court in a large building which we described as a "New Deal Babylonian Temple," located on Capitol Street, facing Capitol Square.

My first assignment was a classically ignominious one. The Utah Genealogical Society, an entity of the Church of Jesus Christ of Latter Day Saints, headquartered in Salt Lake City, Utah, was doing on-site microfilming of the Circuit Court records in the older counties of Virginia. Eight of these counties were established in 1632. Every reel of that microfilm had to be checked for quality control and to make sure the reel contained the contents listed on the box label. Thus I spent many hours with my head poked in the hood of a 1950 microfilm reader.

While I was still a student at R-M, I had been taken numerous times to the Sunday evening gatherings of the Young Adult Fellowship (YAF) sponsored by the Ginter Park Presbyterian Church (GPPC), which worshiped in Schauffler Hall of Union Theological Seminary in Virginia, not to be confused with a seminary of a similar name in New York City.

The YAF was an ecumenical group of young professionals who had migrated to Richmond after the Second World War to work and attend graduate school. It was organized by a small group of members of GPPC and included a young woman named Mary Hood.

Needing and wanting social contacts, I immediately joined the group and became quite active. I still had an ongoing relationship with a young woman whom I had met four years earlier but that was a seesaw affair if there ever was one. It made the stock market seem boringly stable. I tried dating other women but that wasn't very productive either.

Meanwhile, my father was terminally ill and I was back and forth to Norfolk. One of my greatest blessings is that I took a month's leave without pay and slept every night on a gurney in his hospital room until he passed away on April 24, 1951, at the age of 65. He is buried at St. George's Episcopal Church, in Pungoteague.

After his death, I turned my attention full force to my duties as an archivist. There were no classes or workshops – it was strictly on-the-job training. I set out to learn everything I could, not only about the technical side of the profession but also about the vast archival holdings at VSL. The State Archivist was competent and well-motivated but had a serious health condition. His principal assistant was the chief operating officer, saddled with the task of actually running the division on a daily basis. So, I set out to learn the collections, many of which were not described adequately, much less catalogued.

Social life in this country changes so rapidly and dramatically that the past is difficult to describe much less understand. For example, in the 1950s it was typical for young people to get married right out of high school or college. Women's colleges as a rule did not permit students to be married. A young woman who didn't have an engagement ring by Christmas of her final year was apt to be susceptible to a malady called "senior panic."

On December 2, 1951, I turned 26 and was not engaged, much less married. I shared the second floor of a private home with two friends who were in much the same situation. Perhaps I was experiencing a touch of post-senior panic. There is a late 19th century hymn, by Eliza E. Hewitt, entitled "Will There Be Any Stars?" The key line is "Will there be any stars in my crown?"

So, a friend and I, mildly pessimistic about our prospects, wrote a satirical parody, "Will There Be Any Girls Left For Me?" Fortunately the lyrics have not survived.

Happily for both of us, the answer to the question was that we met two wonderful young women with whom we respectively shared rich and fulfilling lives.

As part of my campaign to find the right girl for me, I purchased two season tickets to a schedule of concerts called the Celebrity Series, given at the cavernous Mosque Auditorium. One of the scheduled concerts was nearing and I telephoned Mary Hood and invited her to be my guest. The date was April 4, 1952, and the celebrity guest was the noted pianist, Artur Rubinstein.

I cannot say it was love at first sight yet I was very definitely attracted to her. We were active in the YAF and had been together in the same group many times and in various settings.

What struck me the most is that she was definitely NOT a Southern belle. Rather she was smart, well-educated, articulate, straightforward and sensitive. She was, in many wonderful ways, her own person. From the perspective of 2009, she was liberated, and far ahead of her time. She had a good mind, she enjoyed using that mind, and she intended to continue doing so.

I knew something about her situation but not all that much. Yet when I drove up to Mapleton, the family estate in the Ginter Park section of Richmond, I knew instantly that she and I were from different worlds.

Mary's family situation was quite different from mine. She was an only child, her father was an only child, and her grandfather, William Taylor Hood was born in Chester County, Pennsylvania, and moved to Richmond at the end of the American Civil War. Thus she had no Hood relatives in Virginia, although she had cousins of varying degrees in Pennsylvania.

Her mother, Annie Collins Hood, was born in Caroline County, Virginia, in 1886. The family is described in considerable detail in History of the Collins Family of Caroline County, VA and Related Families 1569 - 1954, by Herbert Ridgeway Collins.

Annie Collins Hood had a half-sister, Ellen Collins Hubbard, who was absorbed into the Hood household at an early age, yet never adopted legally. She and Mary were about the same age and grew up together.

This branch of the Collins family was quite prolific. Annie Collins was from a large family, as was her father. Two siblings, Beatrice Collins Ambrose and Clara Collins Gordon, lived within walking distance of Mapleton, the family estate, and a third sister, Rebecca "Rebe" Collins Jackson lived in the nearby town of Ashland. These aunts of Mary's, and their families were the relatives with whom we had the most sustained contact.

After Mary's grandfather, known in the family as Taylor, moved to Richmond, he went to work for a plant nursery. He eventually acquired the firm, thereafter known as W.T. Hood and Company. He was a pioneer professional nurseryman, of the same generation as Liberty Hyde Bailey, and was the second president of the Southern Nurserymen's Association, in the early 1900s.

W.T. Hood and his wife, Annie Belle Williams Hood, had only one child, Kent Williams Hood, born in 1884.

The original nursery property was in what is now the Ginter Park section of Richmond and the large house was probably built about 1895. It was demolished quite some years ago.

Kent W. Hood married Annie Judith Collins in 1924 and they had only one child, Mary Rawlings Hood, born January 2, 1926.

Kent W. Hood passed away in 1936, when Mary was ten, and Annie C. Hood never remarried.

So, Mary was the only child of a very substantial family and brought a blue collar kid from the wrong side of the tracks home to meet her family. From the day of her birth to the day of her death, Mary never had the slightest financial problem.

Fortunately, good manners and good judgment prevailed and the relationship grew and deepened through the spring and summer.

Mary graduated from the Women's College of Duke University in 1947, returned to Richmond to live at Mapleton and took a position in the foster care program at The Children's Aid Society. Well-situated young women of that era often went into social work of one form or another.

She had taken some graduate courses at Richmond Professional Institute and prior to our first date she had been accepted at the New York School of Social Work, where she hoped to earn a Master's degree. She had arranged to live at International House.

During the academic year 1952 - 1953 I was in Richmond and she was in New York. I visited her there at Thanksgiving and when she came home for Christmas we became engaged.

There were the expected, commonplace rumors that I was marrying her for her money. No way! Anyone who thinks that is a fool of the first order. We did however have very thorough discussions of the financial situation, especially in the event that I would outlive her. Her father's will was classically ambiguous as to what would happen upon her death. We agreed that I would make every reasonable effort to have the estate pass to our surviving children, if any.

Mary was awarded the degree of Master of Social Work (MSW) in 1953 and the wedding was set. One thing should be noted here, because it has a bearing on future events.

My interest in the ministry as a calling, probably present in my life since adolescence had resurfaced and I was considering enrolling at Union Theological Seminary to prepare for ministry in the Presbyterian Church.

Mary told me, candidly and sensitively, that I would have to make a choice between the Presbyterian ministry and marriage with her. That the two would never fit together. That she simply could not be married to a Presbyterian minister.

The result of this was by far the smartest, wisest, most astute decision of my entire life. I chose her, rather than ministry in the Presbyterian Church We were married on August 8, 1953, at the Ginter Park Presbyterian Church. We spent a week at Skyland Resort in Shenandoah National Park. We had a lovely suite with a view of the majestic Shenandoah Valley, one of my favorite places on the planet. The suite was expensive and we ate the cheapest items on the menu in the dining room. We joked about that for many years. Starting a shared life together, we really weren't as limited as we thought of ourselves as being.

(6) "THOSE UNITARIANS DON'T EVEN HAVE A DOCTRINE OF IMMORTALITY"

Mary resigned her position at The Children's Aid Society of Richmond and obtained a job as a School Attendance Worker with the Richmond Public Schools. We rented a garden-style apartment in a post-war housing development called Laburnum Manor, north of Ginter Park and near the Virginia State Fair Grounds. Most of our social friends were active in the Young Adult Fellowship. The group had several married couples so we continued our participation.

Inspired by my parents' success as equal partners, we made a commitment to do the same and successfully sustained our promise for fifty-one years. We pooled our salaried income and paid our living expenses from one bank account. We paid the same respect to each other's information, thoughts and opinions as we gave to our own. This is not easy or simple but with two intelligent, strong-willed individuals it is undoubtedly the best and wisest road to travel. I have serious doubts that any other course of action would have worked.

During the summer of 1954 Mary became pregnant. She resigned her job and never worked for salary another day in her life.

Mrs. Hood (never once did I ever call her "Annie" or any other name) was excited about becoming a grandmother. She had provided us with a lovely wedding and reception but had never actually presented us with a wedding gift. I think she was waiting for the right moment. She gave us a house! Yes, you read that correctly.

She set a dollar range of "probably not more than X," told us to go and find a house, at which time she would write a check. Try that one for size. A recently married couple, expecting their first child, are about to acquire a nice house, as a wedding gift. No rent payments. No mortgage payments. Fifty-five years later I still have trouble getting my head around the generosity of her gift. With the exception of four years when we were living in Canada we were together for fifty one years and never made a mortgage payment.

We found a nice two story brick house on a double lot, about two blocks north of Mapleton and took possession on January 1, 1955.

Kent Hood Evans was born on March 18, 1955, at the Medical College of Virginia, with a severe cleft lip and palate.

This was a difficult experience for us, far more difficult in 1955 than in 2009. Some of our well-meaning yet traditional relatives reacted quite negatively. Mary would have none of that! Every other aspect of his selfhood looked quite normal and healthy and he was OURS! Everything would be just fine. Within minutes we were visited in her hospital room by Dr. Leroy Smith, a well-known and highly respected plastic surgeon who was born with a cleft lip. He and a nurse brought infant Kent to the room and Dr. Smith explained the long, difficult yet promising road that was ahead, immediately and in the future, until Kent was an adult.

Mary's reaction was, "Let's get on with it." It was then, in that context, that I began to think of her as a Titanium Magnolia, my favorite description of her.

You've heard about Steel Magnolias. Yet Mary was stronger than steel, which is the case with titanium.

She had a will, a determination, a resolve to get on with it, no matter how serious the situation or what "it" happened to be.

Were we faced with struggles and adversities? Yes, many. I knew, however, at this point, after less than two years of marriage, that she was made of strong stuff. This proved to be one of the determining factors in our shared life together. Her resolve was greater than mine.

Because Kent had no suction, we had to feed him with a Breck

Feeder. This took a very long time indeed and I recall vividly many hours in a Kennedy rocker, putting the milk into his mouth slowly and carefully. He required several surgeries yet my memory of them is not clear.

Housekeeping was not Mary's favorite activity so we had a housekeeper full-time, forty hours a week, but they did not live in. They were African-American women. She paid them well, provided them with sick leave and vacation and paid all FICA (Social Security) taxes. She related to them kindly and respectfully as employees, not servants.

Once Kent's lip and palate were closed, he just carried on as a normal young child and he continued in that mode throughout his life. He never felt sorry for himself and never saw himself as being different from anyone else.

Mary had serious problems with her second pregnancy, the precise nature of which was never determined. In any event, David Marvin Evans was born July 13, 1957 at Richmond Memorial Hospital, which was close to our home in Ginter Park.

* * *

Meanwhile, serious political, civic and social events were occurring in Virginia and throughout the country. Before long, these events would change the course of our lives.

On May 18, 1954, the United States Supreme Court brought down its unanimous decision in Brown vs. The Board of Education [of Topeka, Kansas] the so-called "school cases." This decision effectively declared that racial segregation in public education was unconstitutional, and had to be discontinued "with all deliberate speed."

The U.S. Supreme Court had combined five cases into one docket. One of those cases involved a suit brought in Prince Edward County, Virginia, in the black belt known as South Side Virginia.

Thus the Commonwealth of Virginia was involved quite directly in the decision and in the consequences of the decision.

From my perspective, both then and now, the civic, religious, social and political leadership of the state simply went berserk. They simply abandoned reason and logic as basic tools for decision-making.

Under the totally misguided leadership of United States Senator Harry Flood Byrd, they vowed that not one black student would ever enter a while class room in the Commonwealth of Virginia. Never! …and never meant never.

The history of this cruel farce, which they called "Massive Resistance," is well-documented in many books and articles.

The atmosphere in Virginia of Massive Resistance was extremely cruel and repressive. So-called Christian churches were at the head of the parade, extolling the same passages from the Holy Bible that they had used to defend slavery. So-called "white" people were doing heinous things to so-called "black" people, and to each other.

The reality was that it created an impossible situation for Mary and me. We knew precisely where we stood. "Justice, equity and compassion in human relations" means what it says, and the pigmentation of one's skin, or such things as ancestry and creed and lifestyle are not factors in the equation.

Virginia was prepared to abandon public education and did abandon it in several localities.

Mary immediately joined the leadership of the Richmond Committee to Save the Public Schools. The only available venue for that brave, fledgling group – the only place where they could discuss strategies, make phone calls and stuff envelopes was at the First Unitarian Church, housed in those days in a small brick church located at the corner of Floyd Avenue and North Harrison Street, in the Fan District. A young man named Eugene Pickett, later president of the Unitarian Universalist Association, was the minister.

We were becoming increasingly isolated socially, except for the people we met in the group described above, many of whom were members of the Unitarian Church.

I was president of the Young Adults of East Hanover Presbytery, yet the Session (Elders) of Ginter Park Presbyterian Church would not let me host the annual meeting at the church because it might be racially integrated. Remember that Mary had been a member of that congregation since she was ten years of age.

This ferment brought forth credo discussions between Mary and me and I discovered, to my amazement, that in spite of her lifelong participation in the Presbyterian church, she was actually a Ralph Waldo Emerson Unitarian. That was clearly and unmistakably the core of her identity.

We became friends with Eugene Pickett and Helen Rice Pickett. She suggested, in a very non-threatening way, that perhaps one or both of us should visit the First Unitarian Church.

My unspoken response was, "Those Unitarians don't even have a doctrine of Immortality."

When I shared this incident with Mary, her response was, "I'm not sure you do either. Leave your theology at home and just go and see what you find."

Finally, one Sunday morning in April of 1958 I made my way to the First Unitarian Church.

Having reflected upon this event for half a century, my feeling is that I had come home to a place that I recognized although I had never been there. Life is essentially a journey to become the person you are meant to be and I was meant to be there. I was home.

When I arrived back at our actual home, Mary had given the boys their lunch and put them down to nap. I think she could sense my excitement. We sat down to our lunch.

"Tell me what happened."

I told her what happened, trying unsuccessfully to restrain my excitement.

What I recall most vividly is that the Service of Worship was about Living in the Here and Now or Living in the 'Transforming Present.' The particular emphasis on justice, equity and compassion in human relations resonated deeply.

The scripture was from great literature other than the Bible. The Liturgy respected my intelligence and my inquiring mind. The sermon was thoughtful and contemporary. It spoke to my needs and longings. The music was relevant and the music director was an African-American man. The prayers were what I call Prayers of Aspiration. Help us to see the need and the ways to live better lives. Here and Now.

By the time I finished, I was quite fired up. We told the story for decades. I still do!

"We should go and join!" Mary exclaimed.

"What?"

"We should go and join!"

"But, I have only been once and you went ten years ago and never went back."

"I know, but if our families learn that we are visiting the Unitarian church, All Hell Will Break Loose. We should 'elope.'

So, we called the church office, made an appointment with Gene Pickett, and when we left his study we had signed the membership book of the First Unitarian Church of Richmond, Virginia.

As was most frequently the case, Mary's assessment was correct. All Hell Did Break Loose, but the 'evil deed' had been done.

We assured our parents, her mother and mine, that we had made our decision and had no intention of turning back. As it turned out, both of them were in failing health and needed us. They had no realistic choice other than to accept our decision.

* * *

We immediately immersed ourselves in the inner workings of the church. The Religious Education Program was bursting at the seams, so Mary applied her talents and energies to that aspect of the program. The compensation package for the minister was woefully inadequate so I eagerly joined an effort to improve that situation.

The congregation numbered about two hundred adults and a large number of children. Families were large in those days. There were five different Orders of Worship, one for each of the possible five Sundays of the month. They reflected particular understandings of worship in a Unitarian context. A mimeographed insert gave the details for each Sunday.

That fall I was elected to the Board of Trustees and in the fall of 1959 I was elected President of the Congregation.

The question arises, quite naturally, as to how I could move, quickly and seamlessly, from being an active Methodist, then a Presbyterian, and from there to being an even more active Unitarian. Just a short time earlier I had permitted my name to go forward as a candidate for the Board of Deacons of the Ginter Park Presbyterian Church. It was a large congregation and fortunately I was not elected. I learned later, while engaged in a research project, that Presbyterian polity condemns Unitarians in harsh, unequivocal language.

The answer, if indeed there is an answer, is found in what I see as the difference between religion and theology.

Religion is about one's search for meaning in life. It asks a variety of questions such as "Who am I, as a person?" "Why am I here?" "What am I supposed to do?" How am I supposed to live my life?

Hundreds of people have said to me, "I'm not religious," or "I'm not very religious."

I have never known anyone who wasn't religious. Even the few hardened, imprisoned people I have known well have addressed those questions at times.

The Religious Quest is basic to consciousness. We simply want to know what Life, OUR Life, is all about.

Theology, by contrast, deals with abstract concepts of belief. Such things as God, Christ, Sin, Heaven, Hell, Resurrection, the list goes on and on.

Very frequently when people learn that I am a retired Unitarian Universalist minister they will ask, almost immediately, "Do you believe in God?" My reply has to be, "Tell me your definition of your God and I will tell you whether you and I have the same God, but I am doubtful because I do not have a God."

There is no normative, universally agreed upon definition of the word God. I have never known two people who had the same God.

Thus the sudden shift from being a Presbyterian to being a Unitarian was about religion and not about theology.

* * *

In terms of the atmosphere of racism that was now so overt in Virginia, the Unitarian church, locally and nationally, had for generations advocated and actualized the religion of Thomas Jefferson, a self-declared Unitarian. Mr. Jefferson articulated that religion extensively in many contexts throughout his life.

The Declaration of Independence sums up the situation quite adequately. ALL people are created free and equal, and are endowed by the Creator with certain inalienable rights, among these being life, liberty and the pursuit of happiness. People of African lineage were being denied their inalienable rights.

I had never in my entire life been unchurched. I wanted and needed a church and, for me, that church was the First Unitarian Church of Richmond, Virginia.

The Seven Principles of Unitarian Universalism were not stated in their present form until about twenty years later, yet the First and Second of those Principles had characterized us for a very long time:

 * The inherent worth and dignity of every person.

 * Justice, equity and compassion in human relations.

* * *

Another major change was emerging on a professional level, a change that would be far-reaching for our whole family.

My 35th birthday was approaching. I had received one promotion at the Virginia State Library yet further advancements were highly unlikely. The two people above me were there to stay. I would never have wanted to be chief of operations and I was not academically qualified to be the State Archivist of Virginia. Most state archives departments were quite small and dominated by an old-boy network that developed after the Second World War. The Federal Government had a much larger archives establishment yet I could never work for them. I am far too much a political junkie. It is in my blood stream.

I did, however, truly enjoy many aspects of my eleven years there. During the early years, prior to the promotion, I rotated on the Reference Desk in the Archives Reading Room. This afforded me the opportunity to interact with visitors, about ten thousand a year.

Many of them were what we called "head hunters" only interested in the names of their ancestors. Others, however, were genuinely interested in the culture in which their ancestors lived.

After the promotion to what was in reality "Keeper of the Collections" I had much greater freedom to choose my projects and how I would use my time.

The lobby contained two very large exhibit cases. I was totally responsible for designing and implementing the exhibits, something I enjoyed very much.

A Guide to Manuscript Collection in the United States was being prepared and I was given the task of preparing the entry for our entire Archives Division, with holdings of an estimated eleven million items.

I especially enjoyed advanced searches for obscure and elusive information. I found that quite challenging.

Things I definitely did not enjoy included packing the records of the defunct, long-existing Tredegar Iron Works. This was far and away the dirtiest job of any kind I have ever done.

All told, I needed to make a change. I enjoyed most of my work there very much but I had no intention of sitting at that same desk for another twenty-five years. I went back many years later to visit and someone was sitting at that same desk doing the same things I had done. I was glad I had realized my bureaucratic limitations.

* * *

Another gift came our way at this time. Mrs. Hood had arranged for Mary to receive an annual income from the Trust Under the Will of Kent W. Hood, established upon his death in 1936.

The amount of this annual payment was such that if we managed our finances carefully, neither of us needed to have any earned income.

We really and truly enjoyed our volunteer work at the First Unitarian Church. I had tried my hand at public speaking and found it to be very stimulating and satisfying. Most importantly, Helen Rice Pickett was most definitely not the traditional preacher's wife. She was an attractive, smart, wise, capable wife and mother whose spouse happened to be the minister of the church. Mary had stated quite emphatically that she could never be the wife of a Presbyterian minister. Inspired by Helen, she thought it would be quite acceptable, even fulfilling, to be the spouse of a Unitarian minister.

And it had become very clear that we wanted to leave the Commonwealth of Virginia – even though Mary had deep roots there, on her mother's side and I had even deeper roots on my father's side.

It is accurate to say that Mary and I simply marched to a different drummer. We simply did not belong in Virginia. Subsequent events have shown our analysis to be quite correct. We could never have had such a rich, interesting, fulfilling life, individually and together, had we not moved.

We began to explore the possibility that I would matriculate at one of the three theological schools: Harvard Divinity School, a division of Harvard University, in Cambridge, Massachusetts; Starr King School for the Ministry, in Berkeley, California; and Meadville Theological School, affiliated with the University of Chicago Divinity School.

Gene Pickett was a graduate of Meadville, and the president and dean of the school was an acquaintance of mine so I decided to enroll at Meadville in the fall of 1961.

I resigned my position at the Virginia State Library and as president of the First Unitarian Church. Friends found us an apartment in Hyde Park, near the school. Mary and I and the boys, ages six and four, made the trek to Chicago, complete with a baby grand piano and a vast accumulation of stuff.

The years in Richmond as a family were, on balance, good years. We had a comfortable house, located quite near Mapleton. The estate still had a cook-housekeeper so we frequently ate dinner there, especially during the week.

Mary had full-time household help and enjoyed outside activities, especially the League of Women Voters. Life was good. It just needed to be different.

Shortly before we were scheduled to leave Richmond, one of the two daily newspapers, probably the Richmond News-Leader, sent a young reporter out to the house to interview us. The resulting article, complete with a very nice photo of the four of us, resulted in a headline that brought us laughs for decades. I still chuckle when I read the article.

Archivist to Leave 'Ivory Tower' Life

Every day at 8:15 a.m., Monday through Friday for the past 10 years, a tall thin bookish-looking man has gone into the Virginia State archives.

Every day at 5 p.m., he has emerged. As an archivist, he has spent the day quietly, working with records the museum is preserving and seeing only an occasional other person, another librarian or researcher.

This week, with a slow smile and a little glint of excitement, Marvin Evans, 35, told an acquaintance, "I'm going to come down from my ivory tower."

This fall ... Evans, his wife, Mary, and their two little boys will set out for Meadville Theological School [at] the University of Chicago....

Evans' decision might seem startling to a casual acquaintance, but many of his friends at Richmond's Unitarian Church are not particularly surprised. They have watched their scholarly friend serve two terms as president of the congregation and have seen, as Evans puts it, his church work become so important "that other things seemed to be getting in the way of what I really wanted to do."

Actually, Evans has felt that the ministry should be his 'life's work' for the past eight to 10 years. The trouble was finding the right church.

His interest began after he came to Richmond and started attending a local Presbyterian church where he met his future wife, then Miss Mary Hood, a young social worker actively interested in church youth work.

Although he started seriously considering the ministry, he couldn't accept all the theological foundations of the Presbyterian Church.

Then one day his wife ... told him about her friend Helen Pickett, wife of Eugene Pickett, the local Unitarian minister.

After [he] visited the little brick Fan District church, Evans knew that "this was what [I] was looking for,"

"Here I found a group of people who are engaged in a quest for meaning in life and who are working out their own personal religion, without any creed being imposed on them," he said.

"Modern man," he continued, "is involved in many quests, quests for solutions to social, scientific, economic and hopefully religious problems."

"The Unitarian church offers a church where the religious quest will never be in conflict with the other quests because each [person] is free to believe what [their] own reason, experience and conscience afford." […he added.]

Because he has had the opportunity to observe the role of minister from the vantage point of president of the congregation, he has formed certain definite opinions of what a minister should be.

The minister, he says, should not be just a good organizer or preacher. He should be "what the name implies by dedicating himself (sic) to ministering to the needs of the congregation."

He hopes to do this partially by stressing the individuality of each member of the congregation.

"In present society, man (sic) is less and less an individual and more and more a member of a group. My wife and I want to work with people in their drive to count for something as individuals."

"The church can serve an important role in this," he said, "by giving a group of individuals an opportunity to draw on the deeper insights of those with whom they associate" and to "defend and articulate their own ideas in free discussion."

Asked if he thought he was going to have difficulty dealing with people face to face after being in an "ivory tower" so long, Evans said, thoughtfully:

"I've thought about that, but I think it will take care of itself."

(7) OFF TO CHICAGO AND SEMINARY

We arrived in Chicago and found that the apartment arranged for us by two students I had met when I visited earlier was in a good location but had some problems. It was in a large building owned by Chicago Theological Seminary (CTS) a school in Hyde Park operated by the United Church of Christ. The apartment was old and dirty and little maintenance had been done over the years. The various schools in the area, principally the large and wealthy University of Chicago, had bought old houses and apartment buildings and were renting the units to students.

The building had settled badly. The floors sloped, only in different ways from room to room. We settled in and Kent enrolled in grade one at Ray School.

Meadville Theological School (MTS) had a very small student body, perhaps thirty students or so. I do recall that the entire student body and faculty could gather in the Curtis Room, a large drawing room in the main building, located at 5701 South Woodlawn Avenue.

Most of the students were in their twenties, some were married, and several had children. In sharp contrast to the situation in 2009, when many men and women turn to the ministry in mid-life, there were only three of us who were older, in our thirties. One had an earned doctorate in chemistry, one had been a very successful Christian Science Practitioner, and I had been an archivist and research historian.

When I visited the school prior to deciding to enroll, I talked with the Dean, Malcolm Sutherland, Jr. about spoon-fed learning because it simply did not work well for me. However I was on a full-tuition scholarship so the decision was made that I should enroll for a full course load during the first quarter.

MTS had long operated in the context of a complex contractual relationship with the University of Chicago. Students were required to gain admission to the Graduate School at UC, after which you were admitted to Meadville. Theoretically, this entitled you to take courses anywhere in the university but in reality most courses were taken at the Divinity School. This was and is an excellent school, with a primary emphasis on degrees at the M.A. and Ph.D. levels.

Meadville was accredited by the Association of Theological Schools and offered some courses in such fields as Unitarian history and polity. However, the core of the requirements for the degree of Bachelor of Divinity (B.D.) was the successful completion of five comprehensive examinations offered by the Divinity School at the end of each academic quarter. The course work was designed to prepare one for taking the "comps." You were not required to take the comps in any particular order or at any particular time. It was a well-nigh perfect formula for procrastination and many students avoided them like the plague.

In any event, I suffered through the first quarter and demonstrated that I was capable of being spoon-fed. However, I was thirty-six years of age, with a spouse and two children, living in a cold environment that I didn't particularly enjoy, and I simply wanted to earn my degree and get out of there. Years of going to class and listening to stale, boring, esoteric lectures simply did not appeal to me. Not my cup of tea.

I explained this quite objectively to Dr. Sutherland and was given permission to study independently. All UC wanted was full tuition, which Meadville paid each quarter.

Extensive bibliographies for all of the comps were readily available, as well as the contents of many of the actual exams. If you were seeking a master's degree or a doctorate you needed to make a fairly high grade. If you were a peon working for a bachelor's degree you only needed to make a passing grade.

I had an excellent academic record in undergraduate school yet I had no interest in one of the advanced degrees so my aim was to pass the exams and obtain my degree.

Meadville had an excellent library, presided over by Dr. Margaret Beall, and I was given full access, twenty-four hours a day, seven days a week, including holidays.

I embarked upon a crash program to complete the comps and accomplished that in twelve calendar months. It was a very interesting experience for me, a very good student, to take five examinations with the sole objective of making a passing grade. I had never done that in my life. I don't recall having done particularly well on any of them. My personal physician pointed out to me many years later that some of the best lawyers, physicians, architects and so on finished in the bottom half of their class in the quest for their professional degrees.

Much to our relief, Chicago Theological Seminary announced that the building in which we were living was being demolished to make room for faculty housing. Mary and I found a very nice third floor walk-up on the South Shore and moved there in May of 1962.

Moving out of Hyde Park definitely reduced our participation in the social life of the school community. We had to drive several miles to get there.

I was obviously not privy to the discussions in the faculty, yet I have a feeling they were uncertain what to do with me at that point. I had completed the requirement for the Bachelor of Divinity degree. In any event I was assigned to a pioneer program in Clinical Pastoral Education (Chaplaincy) at Billings Hospital, the teaching hospital operated by the University of Chicago.

I was also assigned to limited field work at the First Universalist Church of Chicago, under the mentorship of a very recent graduate of Meadville, and also to a one-on-one seminar with Dr. John F. Hayward. The primary objective of this seminar was for me to write a mini-thesis setting forth my philosophy of living and my concept of ministry.

Nothing was said as to what, if anything, would happen if and when I completed these assignments. I was, after all, only in the second year of what was normally a four year program, including a one year full-time ministerial internship, usually away from Chicago.

This gave me the much-needed opportunity to give careful thought and reflection to what I believed, if anything, and why and how I viewed my beliefs.

While Mary and I were members of First Unitarian in Richmond, our contributions were what I call "doing church." She was active in the Religious Education Program. I served on the Board of Trustees and as president of the congregation. Both of us had done this kind of volunteer activity for many years.

Yet Gene Pickett's sermons were thoughtful and provocative in the finest sense. Scores of thoughts and ideas were being planted in my very receptive mind. The quality of his presentations was a core aspect of my motivation to go to theological school. My life was being changed far more deeply and dramatically than I realized.

When I arrived at Meadville, I was immediately called upon to articulate thoughts and ideas I either didn't have or to which I had not given much thought. Now I realized that my Methodist vocabulary would not work if I aspired to speak to Unitarian Universalist congregations. To be effective and authentic in this calling, I had to search for, formulate and develop an understanding of life and an approach to living that was far different from my Methodist upbringing but no different from what I was actually experiencing.

The Meadville Community was, and still is, a good venue for such a journey. Intellectual ferment was embodied in the very nature of a theological school not tied to any particular creed. Although the school prepared students primarily for the Unitarian Universalist Ministry, it was, and still is, an independent corporation.

The great early twentieth century philosopher of religion, Henry Nelson Wieman, had retired in Carbondale, Illinois, but offered a weekly seminar at Meadville. His basic concept, which he called "creative interchange," is too complex to explain here but is available in his various books, including Man's Ultimate Commitment.

I wrote the paper but for the life of me I am unable to locate a copy. It was done hurriedly and saying it was not noteworthy is an accurate statement. It was essentially an elaboration of the basic point I had made to the newspaper reporter who interviewed me prior to leaving Richmond.

However, the exercise of writing the paper again pointed me in the direction of Living in The Transforming Present.

One incident that still amuses me was that after I had completed the paper I had one final seminar session with Professor Hayward, who was also a personal friend.

He said, "Well, I am delighted that we have finished our work together. Congratulations!"

Then, referring to the ideas set forth in the paper, he said, with a twinkle in his eye, "You know what this is?"

Somewhat sheepishly, I replied, "What?"

"The theology of Mammy Yokum."

"How so?"

"Good triumphs over evil, because it's better."

Not to be outdone, I replied, "Yes, I believe that. The historian in me tells me that those of us living today are better off than if we had lived in 1463."

We exchanged a handshake and my work at Meadville was essentially completed.

Shortly after that, Dr. Sutherland called me into his office and informed me that I had been placed on the Commencement List.

I can honestly say, almost fifty years later, that this came as a real surprise to me. I still don't know what happened and even later when I was elected to the Board of Trustees of the School, I never inquired. As a friend of mine, a former deputy prosecutor for the King County Superior Court was wont to say, "Don't ever ask a question unless you know the answer." I definitely did not know the answer and I definitely did not ask the question.

Mary and I were stunned. Such a turn of events was quite rare indeed.

* * *

What to do next?

Dr. Sutherland arranged for me to go to the headquarters of the Unitarian Universalist Association in Boston and be interviewed by the Ministerial Fellowship Committee. Technically I needed to be granted Preliminary Fellowship in the Unitarian Universalist ministry before I could properly seek a position as a UU minister.

I should note here that in 1961, the American Unitarian Association and the Universalist Church of America merged and became the Unitarian Universalist Association. Some individual congregations took the merged name, "Unitarian Universalist" and some didn't.

Today there are exhaustive requirements and extensive forms and affidavits and a long and arduous procedure which requires declaring one's intentions months or years in advance.

All I remember is boarding a train, meeting with the committee late at night when they were tired, returning for a second interview the next morning, and being granted the Preliminary Fellowship.

The usual procedure in those days was to prepare a very elaborate packet of materials of all sorts and then hope that the Department of Ministry would include you on the so-called "Recommended List" which they would then send to one or more congregations that were seeking a minister and had established what was then called a Pulpit Committee, now called a Ministerial Search Committee.

For reasons I cannot articulate to this day, that procedure just didn't appeal to me. Mary and I did not quite know what to do next. We had signed a second one year lease on our apartment. David would turn six on July 13 and be starting grade one in September.

We knew we wanted parish ministry. We knew we wanted a growing, developing situation. We wanted progress and action. We knew we didn't want a moribund church in the northeast. The UUA had and still has a more than adequate supply of those, and we knew we didn't want to be in a cold climate. Two winters in Chicago was more than enough.

Meadville in those days had vespers several evenings a week in Hull Chapel at the First Unitarian Church, located diagonally across

Woodlawn Avenue from the main Meadville building. On Friday evening there was a full Service of Worship, conducted by a faculty member or a student, followed by supper at Meadville House, which served as a small student union for the school community.

One Friday evening as Mary and I were leaving Hull Chapel to go to Meadville House, we were quietly motioned aside by Dr. John Brigham, who was on the staff of the Department of Ministry.

Dr. Brigham related to us that he was returning to Boston after a business trip to Seattle. While in Seattle, he had met with Rev. Peter Raible, who was the part-time District Executive for the Pacific Northwest District, in addition to being the minister at University Unitarian Church in northeast Seattle.

Mr. Raible spoke to Dr. Brigham about a Unitarian congregation in Victoria, British Columbia, Canada, on Vancouver Island. They had recently participated in a program designed to prepare them to seek their own minister. The program went quite well yet did not produce nearly enough pledged income to enable the congregation to call a minister. Further, Mr. Raible deemed the situation to be quite promising if the congregation could get over that hurdle. They had the required membership of sixty-five families and a high level of enthusiasm.

Dr. Brigham mentioned to Mr. Raible that a Meadville student was just finishing his degree and that he and his wife were seeking just the kind of opportunity that seemed to exist in Victoria.

Neither Mary nor I knew anything about British Columbia yet the idea sounded interesting so we gave Dr. Brigham our consent to pursue the matter further.

My understanding, which I never attempted to confirm, was that the Victoria congregation had one name, and only one name. No one else was interested, apparently.

The Unitarian Universalist Association General Assembly met in Chicago, in May, and Mr. Raible interviewed Mary and me on behalf of the Pulpit Committee of the Victoria congregation.

I still wasn't interested in preparing an elaborate packet so I interviewed myself on a Wollensak reel-to-reel tape recorder and mailed the tape to Victoria.

Mr. Raible recommended to the Victoria committee that they invite us to come and "candidate," sight unseen. This is a procedure, usually lasting ten days, when the candidate comes and conducts two services and has many contacts with members, after which they vote as to whether to extend a "call" for the person or persons to be their minister. The same sequence is still used.

My memory is that Mary had never flown in an airplane and was not inclined to do so, certainly not both of us on the same plane. So, we reserved a compartment on the Great Northern Railway's "Empire Builder," We left Kent and David in the care of Professor Hayward and his spouse, Muriel, and headed to Vancouver.

While we were away, Muriel Hayward wrote a delightful letter about the boys.

> Mrs. John F. Hayward
> 7611 S. Merrill Avenue
> Chicago 49, Illinois
> Thursday, June 13 [1963]
>
> Dear Mary and Marvin,
>
> The children have been here a week now, and we still haven't had any troubles. In fact, we're having fun.
>
> Your David is so delightfully sturdy and so comically sure of himself that it's sometimes hard to remember that he is still not six years old yet. I guess it's easy to expect him to act older than he is, but he doesn't seem to mind when I take him down a peg and remind him that he's not the boss. In fact, some of his most disarming grins have been in evidence at such times. He's a real cutie.
>
> And your Kent is so engagingly sweet and cooperative and dependable that I'm surprised when he lets out an angry shout at his brother – which happens most rarely, I must say. I am lost in admiration for an 8 year old who sits down to do his homework as soon as he's home from school, who voluntarily puts on his boots when it's raining, and who volunteers to mow a lawn before anyone mentions that it needs mowing! He's so careful with his things that I think he must be shocked at us careless folk, but he's polite enough not to say a critical word.

David has been a big help to me when I go marketing and do errands – he certainly loves to push and carry things! It's a good thing Mary warned me about his liking to buy candy, for even with that foreknowledge I've been amazed at how much he can eat in the way of sweets. I've set some limits on his between-meal eating simply for my own convenience – I think he would eat every 15 minutes if he had his way. And what amazes me is that he still has room for food at mealtime. What a character!

Kent just came in and offered to take the dog for a walk. The first few days the boys were here, it was obvious that Kent wasn't quite sure of himself with Terry but wanted very much to be friends with him. Now he's Terry (sic) favorite taker-for-a-walker; Terry yips with delight and jumps up on him at the prospect of a walk with him. So they're on their way.

The boys loved the postcards from you. Needless to say, they're hoping for more.

We all hope you're having a good time and finding out many good things about Victoria and the Unitarians and Universalists there. And I hope Mary is feeling fine!

As ever,
Muriel

We were met in Vancouver by the president of the congregation and his spouse, and taken by car to Tsawwassen to board the B.C. ferry across to Swartz Bay, outside Victoria.

The trip across the Strait of Georgia and through Active Pass and the Gulf Islands was the most beautiful sight I had ever seen. I absolutely fell in love with it and am even more in love with it forty-six years later.

The candidating experience went well and we agreed that I would begin my ministry there on September 1. The vote was taken on June 9th.

Two weeks later, back in Chicago, we collected Kent and David and drove to Richmond where I was ordained to ministry by the First Unitarian Church on June 30th.

July and early August flew by as we prepared to move. We entered Canada at Emerson, Manitoba, very late at night, and drove the TransCanada Highway, the final section of which, over Rogers Pass in British Columbia, had recently been completed.

(8) BEHIND THE 'TWEED CURTAIN'

We arrived in Victoria on a Thursday. We were in a bind because a moving van with almost all our worldly goods was still on the way. We had to either find a house to buy or rent, or else put everything in storage.

Mary had many talents and skills and laudable traits, yet shopping, of any variety, never appealed to her. I never knew her to really shop for anything. Together, we bought three houses, four boats, and several cars. The sequence was always the same. Look at a few, a very few indeed, and say, "I'll take that one."

We looked at a few houses on Friday and on Saturday morning bought the first one we had seen. It was a nice, attractive tri-level at 908 Deal Street in the Municipality of Oak Bay. In those days, less so in 2009, Oak Bay was still quite British and was aptly described by residents as "Behind the 'Tweed Curtain'" or perhaps one of the last outposts of the British Empire. People who had lived and worked abroad especially in China and Kenya had retired there.

The house, which is still standing, had an entrance hall on the street level. This level contained the living room with a dining area and an eat-in kitchen. A few steps up led to three bedrooms and two bathrooms. A few steps down led to a family room, a nice den or bedroom or office, a utility room and a two piece bathroom. There was an attached carport. Deal Street at that end was a cul-de-sac with very little traffic. It was one block from Beach Drive and the Oak Bay Beach Hotel and the Oak Bay Marina, and adjacent to the lovely Victoria Golf Club.

That section of Oak Bay was largely a single-family neighborhood. The condominium apartment buildings, many with retail space at street level, had not been built.

Newport Avenue had a small Italian Tailor shop, presided over by Joseph Grosso, who made the most beautiful tailored suits I ever owned before or since, Caspersen's Bakery, the Oak Bay Pharmacy, and a few other shops.

Farther along, on Oak Bay Avenue, we had a classic hardware store, a branch of the Bank of Nova Scotia, and Wright's: Purveyors of Fine Meats to the Nobility and Gentility of Victoria (or was it Oak Bay?)

The Oak Bay Marina had been built and it included a very fine restaurant. The famous Undersea Garden, a floating aquarium, was also there.

We were able to take possession and move in when the moving van arrived on Monday and it's not clear how we managed that. It seems rare in my experience to be able to move that quickly on the purchase of a house. I have a strong feeling that someone contacted the Trust Department of the Virginia Trust Company in Richmond, which had at that point administered the Hood Trust for 27 years, and that someone at VTC said, "If she has signed an acceptable offer for the house, let her move in. Money is not the issue. If the mortgage is not assumable, she can write you a check." For various reasons we assumed the mortgage, the only one we had during our fifty-one years together. Meanwhile we had retained ownership of the house in Richmond as a fall-back position.

Looking back at future developments, I think our troubles in Victoria, which were not related to professional performance, really began that fateful Monday morning.

The members of the congregation knew from Day One that we could afford to come there at 55% of the minimum for full-time ministry because we had independent income. We made no secret of that. We made it quite clear that we would stay three to five years, try to get them into a suitable building and be able to raise the salary up to a minimum level and then we would probably move on.

They knew that. They could see during the ten days we were there that we dressed well, ate well, traveled well, lived well.

Yet from the outset they seemed to resent our life style and the clearly stated goal to increase the minister's compensation to the going market rate so they could replace us when we left. My philosophy was and is that there are two and only two ways to go in this world: Do it as a volunteer, or charge the going market rate. Nothing else works. Don't ever even think about undercutting the market. It's demeaning.

Emigrating to Canada, and especially to Victoria, was hard for us. Neither of us had lived abroad as civilians.

Many people, especially Americans, tend to think of Canada and the United States as quite similar. This is misleading, especially if you go there as a "Landed Immigrant," entitled to live and work in the country.

The institutions of government and law are different in basic ways. There are many cultural differences, not the least of which is deeply-felt resentment by Canadians toward their richer, impetuous, highly individualistic trigger-happy neighbors to the south.

Canadians, or at least those living in Greater Victoria in 1963, still had sharp memories of the Great Depression. They were super-cautious in matters affecting their pocketbook.

The differences impacted us daily, often without any awareness of what was happening.

Shortly after we arrived, people began discussing their social plans for the long Thanksgiving holiday weekend.

"Thanksgiving? That's more than two months in the future, and it always falls on Thursday."

Not so. It is the second Monday in October, and it is a three-day weekend.

The boys were duly enrolled at Monterey School, a public school in Oak Bay. Kent was in grade three and David was in grade one. The school was a classic example of the very slow pace described earlier. The grade three reader had a story about driving to grandma's house for the exciting event of seeing her brand-new mechanical refrigerator.

The situation with the Unitarian Church was difficult. For eight years, 1950-1958, they had been an adult group only. Then, in 1958, they organized a Sunday School, which was held on Sunday morning. A Service of Worship for adults took place on Sunday evening.

When we arrived, the Sunday School met in rented space at 106 Superior Street, in James Bay, a very old section of the city, adjacent to downtown Victoria. The building, owned by the Optimist Club, had been built originally as the Seamen's Institute. It was a home ashore for seamen who found themselves in port or between ships in the days when Victoria was a major port for ocean going vessels.

The Sunday evening Service of Worship was held in quite a different part of the city. It took place at the War Amputees Memorial Centre – commonly called the "War Amps Hall," located at Oak Bay Junction. It was a small auditorium with a large portrait of a very young Queen Elizabeth II hanging on the wall behind the lectern.

The situation was awkward and seemed unworkable yet the first year of one's first ministry is not an appropriate or effective time for major changes.

The congregation wanted to have a proper Service of Installation for their new minister, the first resident full-time Unitarian minister in Victoria in a very long time. So, they rented the lovely Georgian Room at the Empress Hotel and the service took place on Thursday evening, November 21, 1963. The next day, November 22, U.S. President John F. Kennedy was assassinated in Dallas.

Because of long and deep interconnections between the two countries, the tragedy was felt keenly by members of the congregation and by people generally. That Sunday evening, November 25, we mourned his death and celebrated his life.

We navigated our way through the first year, in spite of the inherent difficulties. Having a full-time minister, even an inexperienced one, made a difference and the congregation continued to grow.

The fact that a full-time minister now conducted the service on

Sundays was a major problem. The core group, the people who had been there quite a while, was strictly lay-led. They had a wide variety of guest speakers, read aloud sermons written by various ministers in the U.S. and Canada, held informal discussions, and were visited on occasion by the Rev. Phillip Hewett, who had become the minister of the Unitarian Church of Vancouver in 1956. They liked what they had, and would have preferred to keep what they had. Newer members, however, unmistakably wanted what I call a "Church" experience with an uppercase "C." These two inclinations continued during the entire time we were there and are characteristic of numerous Unitarian congregations with a history similar to the one in Victoria.

During this time, our family settled in relatively well. Kent and David found friends nearby and Mary and I developed friendships that lasted many decades. I will mention only two:

Just as we arrived in Victoria, another somewhat younger couple arrived from Vancouver and opened a small book store on Yates Street, across from what was then the Victoria Public Library. They were Jim Munro and his first wife, Alice – yes, that Alice Munro. Forty-six years later Alice Munro continues to publish some of the finest short stories in the English language, and Jim Monro owns and operates one of the finest small independent book stores on the North American continent, or anywhere else for that matter. Alice's stories and an ongoing friendship with Jim enrich my life to this day.

During "candidating week," the previous June, we were taken to dinner by Blayney and Almeda Scott. They subsequently became fast friends. They had an ex-missionary vessel, Messenger III, and we cruised the coast together for many years. Blayney, the founder of Scott Plastic, Ltd., manufacturers of the famous Scotty Downrigger, was one of my closest friends until he passed away several years ago.

It was also about this time that I acquired my all-time favorite printable description of myself.

The University of Victoria was in its infancy as a full scale university and a delightful young woman, a member of the church, was a student there. The attitude was still widespread, even among teachers in the local high schools, that higher education for young women was a misdirected waste of time, energy and money. She was quite proud of her opportunity to attend university, and went to classes wearing dresses or skirts and stockings and heels.

In any event she was gathering together a group of friends and acquaintances and inviting them to meet the minister of her church, the Not-Very-Reverend Marvin Evans.

A couple years later I finally understood how and why her description appealed to me.

I was at the yacht club one afternoon, strolling the docks. A beautiful new Spencer 35 sloop had just arrived in the harbor. I had met the owners and the man invited me aboard to see the boat. I noticed that as he did that he said something to people who were below in the main cabin.

As I went down the companionway ladder, I smelled beer but couldn't see any glasses or bottles or cans.

I knew instantly what was happening. This was Oak Bay and a minister was coming aboard and they hid their beer.

So, I did what I needed to do.

"Where's my beer? Let's toast this beautiful new boat."

The beers reappeared, along with one for me and we toasted the boat and its owners.

I am sensitive about such incidents to this day. Things have changed in some parts of the United States but not in the south.

I am Pearl's Boy, an ex-blue-collar kid from Norfolk, Virginia who happens to be, among other things a Unitarian Universalist minister. People who know me best say I am an historian and a pleasure boat skipper masquerading somewhat unsuccessfully as a minister – the Not-Very-Reverend Marvin Evans.

* * *

I had long wanted to own a sailboat. When we visited Victoria to candidate in June, I saw a small sailboat riding on a buoy at the Royal Victoria Yacht Club (RVYC) in Cadboro Bay. The boat, owned by a local physician was a CAL 20, designed by C. William Lapworth, one of the early, successful designs of almost fifty designs built in fiberglass and sold under the CAL brand name.

The CAL 20 was being built by a small company in North Vancouver, B.C., under license from the California manufacturer. It was commissioned in May, 1964, and named Shalom. The yacht club, notwithstanding its rather elitist sounding name, was a low-key organization. I was invited to join and became a member. This gave our family a circle of friends and acquaintances, very few of whom had any connection with the Unitarian church.

We leased a berth at the Oak Bay Marina. Mary had never sailed but she and the boys, now 9 and 7, participated enthusiastically in this shared activity that became a way of life for the next four decades.

Another complication related to the church was the fact that the congregation did not have an office of any kind. In fact, they didn't even own a typewriter or a duplicating machine. They had no paid staff other than me. Mailing a weekly newsletter was a major project, not to mention a weekly Order of Worship, maintaining a membership and mailing list, and performing the countless other tasks that are necessary for any organization to function adequately, much less well.

Basically, I was expected to run the church out of my personal office on the lower level of our private home in a residential neighborhood, without a separate entrance. It was difficult to have a private, confidential conversation with a parishioner.

The situation was further complicated by the reality that I can easily be my own worst enemy. I become involved in too many things and set standards I cannot possibly fulfill.

Our congregation wanted to find appropriate and effective ways to be more active and visible in the community. I learned from my counterpart in Vancouver, Dr. Phillip Hewett, minister of the Unitarian Church, that members of that congregation had been instrumental in forming the Memorial Society of British Columbia, or MSBC.

MSBC grew slowly but then two landmark books were published, The High Cost of Dying, by Ruth Harmer, and The American Way of Death, by Jessica Mitford. Reading these books kindled memories of the expensive funerals for my parents, and for many people I had known through the years. I attained some knowledge of memorial societies in Richmond and also while in seminary. The concept became a continuing interest, as will be described later.

Interest in memorial societies increased dramatically and we decided to promote and advocate MSBC in Victoria and on Vancouver Island. I joined the Board of Directors and we were able in due course to establish a branch office and a service facility in Victoria. MSBC is the largest memorial society in North America and Unitarians in Victoria can be justly proud of their pioneering efforts.

The education level of Unitarians is high and ministers are expected to continue their education throughout their career. Preparing a sermon thirty times a year, not based on a text from the Bible, requires extensive reading. This leads some of us to say that we seek "Salvation by Bibliography" or "You Are What You Read."

Reading is central to who I am as a person. I could construct a long list of influential books in my life. One of the books on the list would be "The Feminine Mystique" by Betty Friedan.

It was because of both my mother and Mary that Friedan's book resonated so deeply. Mary was her own person when I met her. In 1964, in Victoria, B.C., or anywhere else for that matter, her situation was replicated by very few other women. On May 30, 1964, my sermon was entitled The Feminine Mystique. It was based partly on Ms. Friedan's book but more particularly on my experiences in a partnership with Mary Hood Evans. The following Sunday, June 7, the topic was The Masculine Mystique. I wrote that out of my head and my seventeen years of friendship and marriage with a wonderful person.

After these sermons, several women in the congregation bonded with one another and over the course of a few years literally transformed their lives and their understanding of themselves as human beings and as women. I remained in close friendship with two of them and rejoiced in their accomplishments.

Obviously it took a long time before The Feminine Mystique began to truly permeate Canadian and American society but I am proud to have been on the leading edge.

* * *

Meanwhile there were some family situations that needed attention. Monterey School was not a good fit for the boys, especially Kent. It was a throwback to the 1930s. Our choices were extremely limited. There were very few options available. Somewhat reluctantly we enrolled them in Glenlyon Preparatory School, a British-type private school for boys, complete with school uniforms and a chauvinist environment, located on the Oak Bay waterfront, a short distance from our home.

Back in the United States, a military incursion in Vietnam was headed toward disaster and the reactionary Barry Goldwater was the Republican Party candidate for president. Mary and I shared a deep interest in politics but could not participate in any way. Yet we had committed ourselves to stay for three to five years so we pursued that goal.

* * *

Finally, some forward progress was made with the church facilities. The decision was made to consolidate all our activities at the Seaman's Institute owned by the Optimist Club and to hold both the Sunday School and the Worship Service on Sunday mornings.

That proved to be a highly advantageous decision.

The building was only being rented from the Optimist Club yet we spent a substantial amount of time, effort and money making it more suitable for our needs.

The stage in the main hall was much too high so we ignored it and arranged the chairs differently. This was not an ideal situation but at least Queen Elizabeth wasn't peering over my shoulders.

The total space was small and we were growing rapidly. Soon we had to move to three sessions of the church school and three worship services, two on Sunday morning and one on Thursday night.

Consolidating our activities at the Seamen's Institute gave some of us, me included, a desire to have permanent premises of our own. Obviously we could not afford that, yet we looked at large old houses, small abandoned grocery stores, and various other places.

This turned out to be excellent preparation for what was just about to happen.

The members of the Optimist Club decided that ownership of the building was not working out for them, and notified us of their intention to offer the building for sale.

This was a major crisis. No one knew of even one viable option remotely adequate to our needs. The congregation clearly did not have the financial capability to purchase the building.

Then it was suggested that a group of us purchase the building, on shares, and own and operate it as a limited company or partnership.

This proved to be feasible and a limited company, Servetus Investments, Ltd., named for the sixteenth century religious martyr, Michael Servetus, was formed. Servetus Investments, Ltd. purchased the building for $30,000 and the transfer took place on February 1, 1966. Because the building was not owned by the church and had other tenants, including the Victoria Operatic Society, it was named "Servetus Hall." Finally, after too many years of wandering around, the Unitarian Church of Victoria had a home.

We were able to make far more extensive modifications, such as tearing out non-load-bearing walls upstairs to make larger classrooms. We established a church office and hired a part-time secretary. Eventually the church acquired ownership of the building, remodeled it extensively, and then sold the property when they moved to their present location on West Saanich Road.

* * *

Because the church had basically no paid staff other than me, sixty to eighty hours was a relatively short week. The church did not hold services during the summer, so Mary and I typically took off during the summer, either aboard Shalom or traveling on our own. I was still working far more than two thousand hours a year but that information did not seem to factor into the equation. We felt we were entitled to a good family life, especially since we were subsidizing the operation to the tune of thousands of dollars a year.

The tipping point came in August, 1966, when Mary's mother, Annie Collins Hood, passed away at the age of 80. The Hood Trust, established in 1936, was invested quite prudently and produced a reasonable annual income, and Mary was the primary beneficiary. She purchased a Ford Mustang and we ordered a CAL 25, both of which we could have done at any time. Also about this time our 1957 Chevrolet station wagon was having problems so we bought a 1967 Dodge Polara 880.

Among the Unitarians, there was an undercurrent of resentment or displeasure as to how Mary was spending her own money.

One evening, over a cup of tea in the living room at 908 Deal Street, Mary suggested quietly that we retire and move to Seattle. That idea had never occurred to me and it came as a surprise. It had been almost a year since Servetus Hall came into being, the minister's salary was slightly above the amount for entry-level ministers and we had accomplished most of what we set out to do.

Even more important was the fact that the United States was in the midst of great social and political upheaval. We could protest, march and write letters and speak out publicly but we couldn't VOTE. We were both citizens of the United States of America with deep roots in our native land, and we needed to get back in our own country and put our oars in the water.

We were required to file income tax returns in both countries. Canada had a surtax on foreign investments, which Mary resented because she had no control over the investments.

Because I was not a citizen of Canada, I could not obtain a station license for a radio-telephone aboard either of the boats. I could not even obtain an operator's license. We regarded this as a serious safety issue. No careful, prudent skipper cruises this coast for weeks at a time, with two adults and two children aboard, without a proper high quality radio-telephone.

So, shortly after January 1, 1967, I informed the Board of Trustees and the congregation that I would resign at the end of the church year and we would move to Seattle.

During Kent and David's spring break at Glenlyon we came to Seattle, staying at the Edgewater Inn on the downtown waterfront. We looked at a few houses and made an offer for one at 1515 NW Woodbine Way, in northwest Seattle.

The CAL 25, named Shalom, as was the CAL 20, was commissioned in May. We sold our house in Victoria, put our household goods and almost everything else in storage, moved aboard the boat, and officially emigrated back into the United States at Friday Harbor, Washington, and then spent the summer on the British Columbia coast as tourists. The boat was new and subject to an import duty, which we paid at Friday Harbor. Mary had not owned her Mustang the required period so she left it in storage in Victoria.

Shalom was not a documented vessel because we were not citizens, so no proper ship's log was kept. We spent a delightful summer in the San Juan Islands and the Gulf Islands. There are many pleasant harbors and coves in that part of the world.

Taken on balance, which is an essential feature of being able to Say 'Yes' to Life the time in Victoria was good. The future of the congregation as a full-service church was no longer in doubt. We helped them stabilize by securing a full-time minister and an adequate if mundane building. Our efforts on behalf of the Memorial Society of B.C. raised their visibility in the community. We demonstrated that after a lapse of many years, the Unitarians had returned to Victoria and planned to stay.

On a personal level, we made many lasting friendships. The boys grew and developed. Kent honed his study habits and enhanced his leadership skills. Both of them took to sailing and David found a lifelong passion.

When the congregation celebrated its 50th Anniversary in 2000, we looked back fondly on a job well done.

(9) THE EMERALD CITY

When Mary suggested that we retire and move to Seattle, both of us had visited the city several times. We liked the geography of the area, nestled between the Olympic Mountains on the west and the Cascades on the east. I especially liked the location on tidal water. The area presented an ambience that appealed to us. The opportunities for sailing were outstanding. We knew we would have access to excellent medical care, especially for Kent's orthodontics which would be extensive and prolonged.

We were due to take possession of our new home in Blue Ridge on August 15, 1967. Located on a high bluff, hence the name Blue Ridge, it has a striking view of Puget Sound and the Olympic Mountains. Finding a home at this location turned out to be very fortunate; we enjoyed it immensely and stayed there for 26 years.

We had visited the University Unitarian Church, founded in 1913. Originally located in the University District, the church had relocated north and east of that location in 1959. They offered me a position on the ministerial staff at the church, quarter-time. I accepted starting September 1 and stayed on for two years.

The Shilshole Bay Marina, located a short distance from Blue Ridge, and operated by the Port of Seattle, had been built a few years earlier. We leased dock space there and were tenants there for more than thirty years.

We were surely misfits in the neighborhood, which was heavily mainstream Christian and heavily Republican. It was an interesting place for us, two very liberal Unitarians and even more liberal Democrats. Mary was always delighted to fill the yard with political signs for Democratic Party candidates and controversial ballot issues.

Although we paid our community assessments and contributed generously to neighborhood projects such as underground wiring and refurbishing a play field, we never joined the Blue Ridge Social Club or attended any of its functions or activities.

School choices for Kent and David fell into place easily. Kent was ready to enter the 7th grade and needed a vigorous environment that would provide outlets for his boundless intellectual curiosity. He needed advance placement courses and opportunities for independent study. We found all we hoped for at Lakeside School, at the time an all-boys college preparatory school, located in north Seattle, several miles from our home. Kent went on his own for a very informal interview and was admitted.

Lakeside was founded so as to bring classic New England prep school education to the "wild, uncultured" Pacific Northwest. The campus in 1967 looked as though it had been picked up by helicopter from a wealthy town in Massachusetts or Connecticut and put down on a hillside just inside the northern city limits of Seattle.

David was bright and capable and with his amiable temperament needed a less structured, person-centered environment.

Fortunately, The Little School had been founded in 1959 by Dr. Eleanor Siegl, who had done her work at Columbia University Teacher's College. At that time the school, which subsequently relocated to Bellevue, WA, used the facilities of University Unitarian Church. David attended the school for grades 5 and 6. Some years later Mary served a term on the Board of Directors of The Little School. Fifty years after its founding it is still a thriving institution.

Mary and I felt, and I still feel, that while the school had an excellent experiential environment, it placed too little emphasis on academics. "When is my child going to learn to read?" was a frequent question posed by parents. In any event, the decision was made to enroll David at Lakeside, in 1969.

David gradually made friends at Lakeside. Much to David's credit he persevered and with special tutoring and full support from many people he made the transition and thus received an excellent education.

Kent's personality was forming, clearly and unmistakably.

Paul Carlson, Class of 1973, was Kent's earliest friend at Lakeside. Paul later wrote a short essay, describing that first year (1967-1968.)

"Kent and I met for the first time when we both came to Lakeside as seventh graders. Neither of us fit readily into any of the groups which quickly formed. We were both shy but became friends... We were both interested in politics of any kind...

"1968 [was] the first election year we really remembered. We shared a few meaningful silly things: in French we marked our answers 'HHH' for right, 'RMN' for half-right, and 'GCW' for wrong. I was happy when I shook hands with Humphrey, but Kent evened the score by meeting Muskie. We campaigned for Humphrey, but Kent was more active than I. We shared defeat and small triumphs the day after the election: Humphrey lost but carried Washington, and [Senator] Magnuson was re-elected.

"We talked on the phone for hours at a time. We said everything and nothing in a wild rambling that occasionally just reaffirmed our friendship without communicating much else."

* * *

Once back in the United States, Mary resumed her interest in the many and varied concerns of the League of Women Voters (LWV) of Seattle. She served on many committees and informal task forces. Unlike many people (me included) she studied prodigiously, read the fine print, and was exceptionally well-informed. She had a particularly compelling interest in social welfare in all its various aspects. She later devoted much time and energy to the Council of Planning Affiliates (COPA), an umbrella organization created by United Way of Seattle and King County.

One of her most useful talents or skills was that she was a good judge of people, and understood their perspectives even when markedly different from her own.

Working on boards and committees, it was frequently this ability that enabled her to figure out what would work or what the group could agree to do, or not do. Her philosophy was to try to do the possible, not the ideal.

The house at 1515 Woodbine Way was built in 1958-59 with a very open floor plan, unlike any other houses in Blue Ridge and unlike any house in which we had lived. In a sense we camped out for the first year. Then in 1968 we engaged an interior designer to help us figure out how to live there comfortably. This proved to be a major project, although when complete, very satisfying. We decided to furnish it in a way that suited our life style, rather than the conventional style that characterized the neighborhood. For example, Mary had her main working desk in the second floor living room that had a ten foot ceiling, a western wall that was entirely glass, and a magnificent view of the Sound and the Mountains. It was a marvelous room, complete with working papers strewn about and huge stacks of The New York Times. A friend who came annually to canvass for the American Cancer Society said it was the only house on her route that appeared designed to enjoy living in and not staged for a feature story in Architectural Digest.

* * *

Retiring from active employment and all-consuming employment at that, at age 41 proved to be much more difficult than I envisioned One's identity as a male and as a useful member of society was defined in major ways by one's job or career. "What do you do?" was frequently an early question when meeting someone for the first time.

I didn't figure out a satisfactory answer until about ten years later. University Unitarian Church, by congregational vote in 1977, gave me the adjunct title "Minister Associated" and I used that title professionally for more than twenty years.

I was elected to the Board of Directors of the Pacific Northwest District (PNWD) of the Unitarian Universalist Association, generally referred to as the UUA. The PNWD at that time comprised Oregon, Washington, northern Idaho, Alaska and British Columbia.

The UUA is a Massachusetts corporation with headquarters on Beacon Hill in downtown Boston. The main headquarters building is immediately adjacent to the Massachusetts State House. In 1969 the voters in PNWD elected me to be their member of the Board of Trustees of the UUA. The organization was in serious financial difficulty and the new administration had to do a major reduction in staff and services.

Even more compelling was the social and cultural upheaval caused by United States incursion in Vietnam, Civil Rights, Black Empowerment and the Women's Movement. These contentious issues were colored by new music (from Elvis to the Beatles), flower children, free love, and LSD.

Closer to home and added to this tumultuous mix, Beacon Press, the wholly owned publishing house of the UUA, published the very controversial Pentagon Papers, in five volumes.

Then, to add fuel to this raging fire, the UUA published a religious education curriculum entitled About Your Sexuality (AYS) in 1970.

The article in Wikipedia, the free encyclopedia, as of November 19, 2009, describes AYS, correctly, as "unique among sex education courses because it used visual materials that depicted human sexuality in a realistic and graphic fashion. For example, film strips used in the course showed images of real heterosexual and homosexual encounters, and masturbation. These images did not try to hide the genitals or the details of penetration..." AYS was considered very controversial (an understatement) at the time of its inception and in the mid-1990s when it was replaced by "Our Whole Lives."

We had scores of dear, cherished friends at University Unitarian Church. The farther out on the limbs we crawled, the more accepting and appreciative they seemed to be. Time and time again we took public positions that were quite controversial. That is why we retired from the ministry so we would have the freedom to do more of what we thought and felt needed to be done.

Even so, Kent was convinced beyond doubt that one dark and stormy night a rap would come on the door and FBI agents would haul Dad away, never to be seen or heard from again.

(10) A COMPUTER ON EVERY DESK

Fly into the Seattle-Tacoma International Airport and rent a car. Drive north on Interstate 5, through downtown Seattle. Continue on several miles to Exit 175, at the northern edge of the city limits. Take the 145th Street off ramp. Turn left, cross back over the Interstate, and at the second traffic light turn left on 1st Avenue, NE.

Continue south on 1st Avenue and turn left at 137th St. Watch for Lakeside Middle School on your right, and park in a Visitors space. Enter the building, turn right, and watch for the Evans Theater on your left. There you will see a wall-mounted plaque which reads:

EVANS THEATER
Dedicated in memory of
Kent Hood Evans '73,
1955 - 1972
by a generous gift from his
friend and classmate
William H. Gates III '73
September 9, 1999

If the theater is not in use, speak to a staff person and see if you can have a quick look inside. It's a versatile space, ideal for lively middle school students.

Return to your car and drive north on 1st Avenue, a short distance. Look for a sign on your right reading Lakeside School at 14050 1st Avenue, NE. Turn right into the tree-lined driveway. Just ahead you will see the center of the campus, called Red Square, the steeple of the beautiful McKay Chapel, and a sweep of other buildings.

Again park in a Visitors space and walk a short distance to the front of the building immediately adjacent to the parking lot. The entrance faces Red Square.

This is Allen - Gates Hall.

Just inside the entrance there is a bronze plaque mounted on the wall:

ALLEN - GATES HALL

**This building, for the study of science and
mathematics, is the generous gift of
PAUL G. ALLEN '71 and WILLIAM H. GATES '73
Dedicated September 25, 1987
In memory of classmate, friend and
fellow-explorer
Kent Hood Evans
1955 - 1972**

Continue walking a few feet to the left and you will see the Kent Hood Evans Auditorium, a very versatile amphitheater style space, one of the most-used facilities on the Lakeside campus.

Exit the building and just to the north of the McKay Chapel you will see the Pigott Family Arts Center. Take the stairs or elevator to Level 2 There, recessed into the wall, you will find a small yet significant exhibit labeled:

**The Birth of
The Software
Industry**

Some years ago, McAlister Hall, which was on this site, was replaced by the Pigott Family Arts Center and this exhibit is located in approximately the same spot as the infamous Computer Room.

There are several explanatory panels included in the exhibit. One of the most prominent of these features is a quote from an interview that Bill Gates gave to the National Museum of American History of the Smithsonian Institution, many years ago. A forty-six page transcript of that interview is available on the museum's website.

If you delve even more deeply, you will find a Kent H. Evans Permanent Scholarship, established in 1973, and a Pocock Rowing Shell named "Kent Evans."

All of these things indicate Kent's impact on other students, faculty and the school itself during his five years there.

Who was this emerging young entrepreneur? What was he like as a human being, a person? Fathers are not the most objective observers yet time has deepened and tempered my perceptions so I will attempt to share my impressions with you.

You will recall that Kent was born with a severe cleft lip and palate. He had numerous surgeries and by the time he entered Lakeside he had a mouth filled with intricate orthodontics. None of this seemed to affect him appreciably, except to make him more sensitive to people with similar imperfections.

Even though we moved from Richmond to Chicago to Victoria to Seattle, I think it is accurate to say that he and his brother had a stable early childhood, during which they loved and were loved, in abundance.

He was always well-dressed, well-mannered and well-motivated. He was the student who received the "Good Citizenship Award" in elementary school. I have tried various one word descriptions of his demeanor over the years, words like conventional, traditional, liberal, conservative and so on, yet the word than keeps coming to the forefront is civilized. He cared about himself, about other people, about the body politic, and about the planet Earth.

Although he always did well in school, he was most assuredly not a genius, and his interests were so varied that I have difficulty thinking of him as simply a nerd. His social skills were exceptional.

No matter what he decided to delve into he proved to be a quick study. He was a self-starter and absorbed knowledge and information quickly. Meanwhile, he fathomed the significance and implications of what he was learning. I recall vividly that during his junior year, we went together to a presentation by a recruiter from Carleton College, in Northfield, Minnesota. After the recruiter finished his talk, he invited questions. Kent stood and said respectfully, "I can get a good education anywhere. What else do you have to offer?"

Lakeside School was unquestionably a good place for Kent. Various writers, notably Stephen Manes, Paul Andrews, James Wallace and Jim Erickson, describe Lakeside School as being elitist and a bastion of education for the establishment in Seattle. That description barely scratches the surface and therefore I see it as misleading. Although our family had an income that met our well-managed needs, we were not wealthy by any stretch of the imagination and we were never for even one moment a part of the Seattle Establishment. Mary and I were both educated in the public schools of Richmond and Norfolk. She had resisted the continued attempts by her mother to send her to Saint Catherine's School, a private school for girls.

The reality of the matter is that the public schools in Seattle were quite unsettled in those days and Mary and I knew from our own experience that middle school and high school are enormously important and formative. We spent our money carefully and wisely in order to send Kent and David to Lakeside, and many other families did likewise. Forty years later, Lakeside is one of the most diverse, inclusive schools, public or private, in this part of the world. Yet the elitist reputation lives on.

Kent's first year at Lakeside, our first year in Seattle, was mostly about the exciting intellectual atmosphere and politics, politics, politics. Mary and I were political junkies and Kent even more so. I recall that one morning at breakfast, probably at a very early hour, he confronted me with an Attitude Test from the American Civil Liberties Union (ACLU).

I was well-acquainted with the policies and positions of the ACLU so I made a perfect score. He was somewhat amazed by that so I proceeded to point out to him that I gave the answers that the ACLU was looking for, but that they in no way necessarily represented what I actually thought about the questions. I then took the test again and gave him my answers rather than the ACLU answers. It was a good experience for him. People frequently tell a questioner what they think the questioner wants to hear, rather than what they actually think or believe.

* * *

My only niece, Nancy Walton, then a young woman of twenty-three, working for the U.S. Food and Drug Administration, still laughs about their visit to Washington D.C. Two precocious, fearless fourteen-year-old boys storming around the U.S. Capitol as though they owned the place.

* * *

What happened in the fall of 1968 is related in many books and articles and has taken on some of the aspects of a legend, part fact, part hindsight and part imagination.

The Lakeside School Mothers Club (now the Lakeside School Parents Association) held a famous annual rummage sale for many decades. Very well-known companies donate vast quantities of goods, as do private citizens. The sale draws huge crowds and is enormously profitable. I recall that Arthur D. "Dan" Ayrault, Jr., who became Headmaster in 1969, was testifying once before a committee of the Washington State Legislature regarding the funding of independent schools. Listing the funding sources for Lakeside he said, "We have an annual rummage sale..." There were a few snickers. "...which last year produced slightly more than one hundred thousand dollars." No more snickers.

The annual rummage sale, and the auction, were major events and resulted in significant allocations which the school could not afford to include in the annual budget.

Part of the proceeds from the 1968 Lakeside Rummage Sale went to purchase computer time.

* * *

Socially speaking, middle school and high school are two very different worlds. What developed was a highly unlikely foursome of two middle school 8th grade youngsters, Kent Evans and Bill Gates and two young men, sophomores in high school, Paul G. Allen and Richard "Ric" W. Weiland, III.

The four boys divided naturally into two competing pairs. High school students by definition lord it over people in middle school and a totally explainable turf war ensued. I cannot vouch for Bill yet I can say without hesitation that Kent was fearless. Even in the context of our family he stated his positions with force and clarity, held his ground, and most often prevailed because his stance made sense. As is frequently the case with people of that temperament, he also had a short fuse. He became quite angry and assertive if he thought he was being wronged, deceived, cheated, or slighted or whatever. He had two well-educated, highly verbal parents yet in his mind he had the same attributes; thus reason, knowledge and logic had to prevail.

* * *

A teletype was leased and placed in a very small room in McAlister Hall. My distinct impression is that the math faculty, which Bill Gates, Jr. accurately described as being intimidated by THE THING, gathered the more proficient students together and said, in effect, here's this THING. See what you can make of it.

Bill puts it this way, in the Smithsonian interview mentioned earlier:

> "The amount of time we'd spend in this particular room that had the Teletype was quite extreme... The teachers thought we were quite unusual. And pretty quickly there were four of us who got more addicted, more involved, and understood it better than the others. And those were myself, Paul Allen, who later founded Microsoft with me, Ric Weiland, who actually worked at Microsoft in the early days, and Kent Evans, who was my closest friend, and most my age... So, the four of us became the Lakeside Programming Group. We were the hardcore users."

Note here the name, Lakeside Programming Group. The name has been widely rendered, in thousands of places, as the Lakeside Programmers Group, but that was not the name.

I am not sure how the name, Lakeside Programming Group originated. I do know from conversations with Kent that they wanted a name that indicated more than a club, such as the Chess Club or the Spanish Club, yet less than a commercial company. It was most definitely a closed group, open only to the four of them. I don't know whether they had a formal written agreement of any kind.

One thing is for sure, this was total immersion. And, as usual, they were fearless. They were on the prowl for information, assistance, computer time, contacts, opportunities, and anything else that happened to be in full view or lurking in the shadows.

A far more definitive history of the Lakeside Programming Group would need to be written by Bill Gates, Jr., and/or Paul Allen.

* * *

Yet an interesting insight as to their activities is found in a journal Kent kept during the academic year 1970 - 1971, obviously as a class assignment. It appears that he was only required to write a specified number of words each week.

This was the final year that the four of them were together at Lakeside. Paul and Ric graduated in June of 1971.

There were at least two significant projects.

On November 23, 1970, Kent writes:

> "It's going to be an interesting experience to teach a course after so many years of taking them. With three friends [Bill, Paul and Ric] I'm teaching a minor called "Introduction to Computer Science" next trimester. If a team of two creates confusion, our group of four will make chaos if we don't watch out.
>
> "Other challenges face us. Most formidable is the lack of an established course curriculum or a suitable text. Lakeside has never before taught a course like this. It looks like we've gotten ourselves into a lot of bibliography searching and ditto master typing. Still, it is going to be fun to get the teacher's perspective on teaching for a change."

Two months later, the mood had shifted.

> "I wrote comments this weekend for the computer science minor I teach. After the novelty of it wore off, it wasn't fun.
>
> "Writing a comment takes me ten minutes, since I've never done it before, so I spent a total of an hour and a half doing them.
>
> "Writing comments on people you know well isn't bad, but judging on the basis of superficial contacts in class is difficult.

We were faced with the problem of assigning tentative grades without any written assignment to go on since about the only thing each student will do is a project in the last few weeks of the trimester.

"Judging your peers for the record and in a hopefully objective manner is painful. It's not like the offhand comments we make all the time. Comments have more serious consequences.

"You've got to be right. Did Jim really skip a lot of classes or is that just the impression he gave you by not showing up once or twice? The class isn't learning as well as you expected. Who's fault is that? Are you failing as a teacher or are they lousy students? Probably both. If that's the case, how can you give them tentative grades?

"We were so unsure of ourselves that we gave all As and Bs. Now we're paying a lot of attention to attendance. If there's one thing we can't stand it's people who don't want to hear our lectures. They're really going to get it, we say to ourselves."

There are no further comments about this course, yet he talked many times about how he set out to learn how to teach and, according to both faculty and students he became an excellent teacher. He was convinced you could learn how to teach.

* * *

Their most important endeavor of that year, 1970-1971, was a huge programming project.

"Since the middle of December, Bill Gates, Paul Allen, Ric Weiland and I have been working on a project for a computer service company in Portland called Information Sciences Incorporated [ISI]. They provide computer facilities and expertise to other firms in the Pacific Northwest.

"Using any teletype terminal (a typewriter-like device that can transmit characters to and from the computer over regular phone lines) you can communicate with Information Sciences' computer. They have a special phone line from Seattle so we don't have to pay long-distance charges.

"We have been writing a very complex computer program to

do customer's payrolls. This is very educational because we've learned a lot about working in a business environment and dealing with government agencies.

"March 16th is our deadline. During the past few weeks we've been frantically trying to get it done.

"Tuesday we go to Portland to deliver the program, and, as they put it, 'hammer out an agreement on future work.' Everything so far has been done for its educational benefits and for large amounts of expensive computer time. Now we want to get some monetary benefits too.

"This morning [we] took the 7:00 Greyhound bus to Portland... We had all put on coats and ties. We thought it was hilarious to be taking Greyhound for a business trip. Well they do call it an Express V.I.P. Executive Coach.

"The bus got us to Portland about 11:00. We walked eight blocks to the company's impressive suite on the ground floor of a new office building.

"Shortly after we arrived we met with Rodger (sic) Bakken, Marketing Manager, Commercial Applications in an office made available for our use. It happens that the customer we're writing our program for doesn't know we're high school students. We needed to ask several questions so Ric Weiland, who sounds oldest, phoned Rogers Organ Company. Bakken said, 'Remember you're with Information Sciences and make twenty thousand.' He paused and added, 'Twenty thousand mistakes a year' Oh well, maybe someday...When we said the program had been delayed two weeks, he said, 'Don't worry about it' Of course, he appended, 'It's just a sale.'

Then they were taken to lunch at an upscale pizza place.

"After we got back to the offices, our work began. We started with a long conversation in the office of Bud Pembroke, the man in charge of the type of work we do. We agreed that there were plenty of things that we could do when the regular staff was overloaded... We were all given pencil and paper and wrote resumes to aid them in hiring us. The resume is probably the most important thing I've written.

"It wasn't over yet. We'd established that there were things we could do but money hadn't even been mentioned.

"[We] didn't want to be paid hourly rates so we suggested piece rates for program products or royalty arrangements. The royalty scheme went over big. We get about ten percent of the money ISI gets because of one of our programs. We get more in the long run and the company doesn't need to tie up any of its capital.

"Finally about five o'clock we had to leave. We picked up our briefcases and walked down the street to find a place to eat before catching the bus back. They had suggested the Hilton and I was for it but Bill chose the Hamburger Train. Not bad, but after a successful day of business talks?

"The trip back was a disaster.

"It [the bus] had windows that can be pushed out to make emergency exits. It sounds nice but doesn't feel to (sic) hot when you're sitting by one that has been dislodged. It was a bit chilly to say the least on a snowy night. No bus again. Next time we'll be sure to take the train."

Kent's in-person account of this adventure was quite animated and entertaining. It became a favorite story and he never let loose of the fact that after a very successful business negotiation they went to Hamburger Train rather than to the Hilton. Kent was his mother's son. He never bothered to look at the right side of the menu in a restaurant.

I suggested that next time they engage a limousine with a chauffeur and a bar stocked with beverages, snacks and adequate food for bottomless pit teenagers and young adults, and travel in the style to which Kent at least would like to become accustomed. He thought that was a fine idea.

* * *

In addition to his account of these exploits, the journal is filled with thoughts and observations about current events, politics, what books he is reading, what plays he is seeing, a camping trip to the Olympic Peninsula with Lakeside students and faculty and an array of other topics.

He included a detailed account of the election of November 3, mentions that he wrote a 750 word paper for Mrs. Stephens in support of Referendum 29 concerning abortion, and includes the text of a letter to KIRO-TV protesting that they have discontinued the CBS Sunday Evening News with Roger Mudd. He observed that, "The technical and political possibilities for a 1984 resembling [George] Orwell's seem to be increasing."

He was also reading and thinking and speculating about the future of computers.

> "A book I have just read, Computers and the Human Mind written by an electrical engineer for the Science Study Series of the Physical Science Study Committee provides a lot of material for thought. It was a lousy book but its premises are considered to be valid.

> "The brain is considered to be a complex but slow organic computer. The brain contains a trillion circuits but only a fraction of these are used for thinking. There is no evidence that there is anything special about the brain.

> "The author gives a multi-faced (sic) definition of intelligence from Webster's Third International Dictionary. Then he describes computer programs which meet some of these criteria. All the criteria are met by some programs but not all by one program yet. Even creativity is simulated by either randomness or trying all the possibilities. Soon (within this decade probably) computers will be programmed to act intellectually. Perhaps within my lifetime the computer's intellectual capacity will exceed ours.

> "What form will this imminent intellectual revolution take? Will the thinking computer be our tool for saving the world? Or will these computers displace us as masters of the world? This may be the stuff of horror stories but this question, the role of computers in society, is one that the computer industry must begin to face now."

While all this was happening, seemingly enough to occupy the full -time attention of a mature adult, there was also the matter of a very heavy course load, some of it in the Honors Program at Lakeside.

For example, he was taking Honors Physics, a college-level course. On June 8th he submitted a 16 page paper entitled, TRANSMIS-SION OF POWER BY LASER FROM A NUCLEAR REACTOR IN EARTH ORBIT, complete with a "Summary of Experimental Por-tion of Physics Project," and a 24 item bibliography. The teacher's comment was, "Great idea – well presented report – Your research is seemingly very extensive." Kent notes that he did much of the research at the University of Washington Engineering Library.

Yet not everything was intellectual or esoteric.

> "I walked into a Federal Office Building ...with my briefcase (that gigantic black monstrosity.) Two guards immediately told me to open it up. (I guess they were particularly nervous be-cause this was outside the FBI office.) When they saw all the books, they told me to leave."

Although deeply involved in computer work, out hiking and climbing every weekend and perpetually behind schedule with his very demanding academic program at Lakeside, Kent treasured his friendships with both students and faculty and somehow always managed to have time for these relationships.

This aspect of his life is expressed very poignantly by Ric Weiland.

> "Whenever I think of Kent...all the things he added to my life come to mind. Besides a very close friendship... Kent gave me an enchantment with sailing and his many other interests. I'll never forget his unique personality - - how diligent he was in whatever he did and yet how friendly, humble and sincere he was in what he did. (Many a time I tried to imitate Kent's behavior, trying to be more like him.) Yes, Kent gave me very much..."

Since Kent did not reach his 16th birthday until March 18, 1971, near the end of his sophomore year and Bill Gates was seven months younger, during most of the first three years of the computer ad-venture, yours truly hauled them around, or they begged rides or rode the bus.

During Kent's final year, 1971-1972, Paul and Ric had graduated and gone on to university, Paul to Washington State and Ric to Stanford. Bill and Kent were now the sole participants in LPG. This was the year in which they negotiated the contract with the school to program all the class scheduling, an incredibly complex matter in a school with an unusually large number of course offerings and other campus activities. Kent's untimely death was what brought Bill and Paul together to fulfill the contract.

* * *

I have been asked many times, for many years, to share my observations about this truly remarkable friendship between two teen-age boys, Kent and Bill. It is important to note than I don't recall meeting either Paul Allen or Ric Weiland until many years later.

I have hesitated to share my thoughts because I was, after all, an observer, not a participant.

Yet this is a memoir, not an autobiography or history. Thus I have considerably more latitude than might not otherwise be the case. My old Funk & Wagnalls Standard Dictionary International Edition defines memoir as "an account of something deemed worthy of record."

I am not an authority on teenage friendships. Yet this friendship between Kent Evans and Bill Gates is far and away the most interesting and far-reaching one I have ever encountered.

Keep in mind that in September of 1968, Kent was 13 and Bill was 12. It was not all that long before it became the mission, at least for Kent, in his own words, to "put a computer on every desk."

My imaginary "equation" for what happened in less than a decade looks like this"

Kent + Bill + Paul +Ric + Lots of Other People = Microsoft.

Their minds, temperament and personalities were quite different. Kent had an inquiring mind. He had a wide-ranging curiosity; he read prodigiously and he connected the dots. He was a quick-study and he thought things through to what he considered to be a logical conclusion.

Bill, by contrast, had what I would call an impact mind. Knowledge impacted his mind and then imploded, sometimes with clarity and other times chaotically, it seemed.

Kent was most often quiet and even-tempered, except when he felt put-upon. I do not recall even one teacher-parents conference that made any reference to anything other than model behavior. He seems to have bypassed virtually all of the typical pitfalls of childhood and adolescence. He was not particularly interested in popular music, rebellion or even girls. His explanation was that he was too busy. Girls, he said, would perhaps come much later because he thought two or three doctorates and a law degree would be quite useful.

The published descriptions of Bill paint a picture of a restless, turbulent, somewhat chaotic childhood, albeit in a very supportive, loving family.

Bill is described as shy and somewhat uncomfortable in social situations. Kent, early on, chose his peer friends very carefully and seemed to be more comfortable when engaged in conversation with adults. He loved talking with all kinds of people about their lives and their interests and how they understood things. When Kent began teaching at the Middle School, the first time he gave a quiz, every student in the class failed. This told him he needed to learn how to teach and he set out to do this in a very systematic, intentional way. This vastly improved his ability to interact with his peers and with the younger students in the Middle School.

Here's what one of those Middle School students wrote:

> "The first day I met Kent, I admired him. The way he stuck up for what he thought was right, and the way he taught me to use the computer, both made me happy... Kent could explain things better than anyone else."

Having written all of the above, with considerable care and even soul-searching, I truly believe that the heart of this truly remarkable young friendship between Kent and Bill is to be found in the somewhat murky waters of creativity and imagination, a world that many of us would love to understand, patent and market. It also speaks to the serendipity of timing and what can evolve when two bright and complementary minds inspire each other.

My feeling, based largely on conversations with Kent, is that separately and together he and Bill engaged in a very high form of creative thinking that has occurred down through the centuries, frequently changing life on this planet significantly and forever.

They did an enormous amount of brainstorming, visualizing, even fantasizing, trying to conceptualize ways to actualize their mission, namely to put a computer on every desk.

There is no question that these two young boys learned the popular programming languages of their day, and wrote complex programs such as the first Lakeside scheduling program, the one they rescued in 1971 before being awarded the contract in 1972.

Yet their ability to write programs and understand technology simply does not account for their vision of putting a computer on every desk and making lots of money along the way. Kent had a business-oriented mind and carried all the major business magazines in his oversized brief case.

Kent did not live to see that mission realized, yet I believe that the friendship between him and Bill was an important, even vital and essential element in the Microsoft story. I still believe that this creative, remarkable friendship is one worthy of contemplation and gratitude.

The friendship carries a poignant message for everyone involved in elementary and secondary education. What happened at Lakeside School during those four years, 1968-1972, was not on anyone's radar. If I had been the head of the math department, or director of the Middle School, what happened would probably not have happened.

Two senior faculty members, Fred Wright and Bill Dougall, in addition to others, were absolutely essential to what happened. Had they reacted and responded differently, it is highly likely that the seeds of what later became Microsoft Corporation would not have been planted at Lakeside, much less begun to germinate.

Fred Wright wrote:

> "The kids had the freedom to go well beyond what we could offer them. One thing we can take credit for is staying out of the way. I quickly figured out at some point they were way ahead of us. I could point them in a direction but if I had any ques-

tions I went to them for technical assistance." He taught math at Lakeside for four decades, and had been there only two years when all this began.

Another key teacher was Bill Dougall, who joined the faculty in 1957 and also taught for four decades. He wrote:

> "Bill and Kent often competed with Paul and Rick (sic) Weiland '71. You could only envy the energy of their years together, the excitement in that room. There was a threat you could hold over their heads, 'If you don't do your homework, you don't go into that room.'"

I cannot give an account for Bill but I know for a fact that Kent not only tied up the phone lines but violated many rules and procedures. He slept in the computer room, skipped physical education, cut classes and went to the Middle School, was late turning in lab books and other assignments. Even worse, he had a healthy yet forthright skepticism regarding the faculty and the administration and how they were running the school.

The Reverend Robert L. Fulghum, at the time Minister at the Edmonds Unitarian Church and Director of Visual Arts at Lakeside, put it this way:

> "The last personal contact I had with Kent was after a faculty meeting when he and his colleagues had presented a plan for teacher evaluation at Lakeside... When I asked him coming out of the meeting what his reaction was to how the faculty accepted the proposal, he said in a very kind and benevolent but slightly humorous way, 'Well, they've got a lot to learn.'
>
> "And, as usual, he spoke the truth."

Mark Leibovich, writing in The New Imperialists, published in 2002, takes the view that at important stages in Bill Gates' life, significant relationships have developed. These relationships were far more than ordinary friendships. They were mentally engaging, highly imaginative and stimulating.

Mark interviewed Mary and me in depth, then interviewed Bill, and returned for a second in depth interview with us.

I agreed to the second interview because Mark was at that time a technology reporter for The Washington Post. He seemed to have a good sense (much better than mine) of what these teenagers were doing at that early time, and a grasp of the creative energy that was flowing in all directions. Sometimes chaotic. Sometimes mistaken. Occasionally outrageous. Yet laser focused and highly productive.

This was, I think, the story of the Lakeside Programming Group. Four teenagers! Out to change the world!

* * *

Kent was enrolled in a mountain climbing class at the University of Washington at the end of his junior year at Lakeside. On the final climb of the course, he fell on Mt. Shuksan in the North Cascade Mountains. He was brought out by a helicopter from the Whidbey Island Naval Air Station and pronounced dead at a hospital in Bellingham, on May 28, 1972.

Marvin - 8th Grade; Army-WWII;
In a nice tweed suit at Randolph-Macon (1946);
Portrait (1967 or '68)

The Chief; Miss Pearl; Marvin, Christine & The Chief; Christine's Wedding; Marvin with parents; Christine & Marvin in uniform 1944

Miss Mary & Captain Eg
Miss Pearl and the Chief at the Tomb of the Unknown Soldier

Tugboat Nonpareil

CRADDOCKVILLE UNITED METHODIST CHURCH

10 generations of Marvin's family have attended this church

Evans House

FIRST UNITARIAN CHURCH RICHMOND, VIRGINIA

Mary Hood
before meeting Marvin

Wedding picture

"Queen" Mary

~~~~~~

Where we "eloped" to join
the Unitarian Church

Looking Ahead: Off to Chicago 1961; Mrs. Annie Hood & Kent
Kent & David; Miss Pearl & David

Mary, Marvin, Kent, Bill Gates, Jr., Jim Munro
Aboard the Shenandoah, 1970

Shenandoah, Yonder, Messenger III, Argonaut II
Mink Island, BC

Kent & Marvin on the
Shenandoah

David

Mary reading
in the wheelhouse
of the Brandywine.
Her favorite spot!

Kent at Teletype

Evans Theater Plaque

EVANS THEATER

Dedicated in memory of
Kent Hood Evans '73,
1955 - 1972
by a generous gift from his
friend and classmate
William H. Gates III '73

September 9, 1999

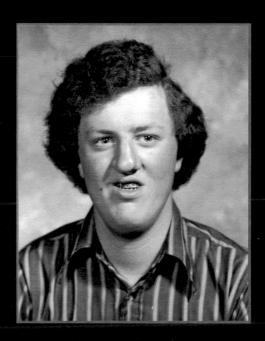

Kent 1972

Allen ◆ Gates Hall Plaque

ALLEN ◆ GATES
HALL
This building, for the study of science and
mathematics, is the generous gift of
PAUL G. ALLEN '71 and WILLIAM H. GATES '73

Dedicated September 25, 1987
In memory of classmate, friend and
fellow-explorer
Kent Hood Evans
1955 – 1972

McKay Chapel - Lakeside School
"Kent Evans" Pocock Rowing Shell, Mary & Marvin

David, Mary & Marvin
Sun Princess Cruise (mid-70s)

Charles & Hazel Mitchell
at Hill Island Marina

Edmonds Community College
Graduation 2008

Alexis Johanson and son Michael
David & Alexis

Mary's Boat "Brandywine" in Desolation Sound
with Mt. Denman visible off the bow

The Bellingham Unitarian Fellowship
a Unitarian Universalist Congregation

recognizes the services of

Marvin Davis Evans

Historian, archivist, minister, wise
counselor, skillful leader and beloved
friend of this congregation,

as its Interim Minister from
1 November 1984 to 31 May 1986,

a time of joyful growth, deepened commitment
and creative excitement in the
life of this society.

Acting upon the recommendation of its Board,
this congregation, by unanimous vote
on 10 April 1988,
does respectfully confer upon him the title

Minister Emeritus

of The Bellingham Unitarian Fellowship
with all the rights, duties, privileges and
honors thereto appertaining, and with the
continuing admiration, love and affection
of us all.

Done at Bellingham, Washington, this
eighth day of May, nineteen hundred
eighty-eight of the Common Era, in
witness whereof we set our hands.

Frank Mitchell
Secretary of the Board

Vera Hagen
President of the Board

Marvin at Lakeside School - 84th Birthday 2009

(11) OUTSIDE THE RANGE OF EXPECTATION

Mary said frequently and with deep feeling that Kent's death was not in the natural order of things. As parents in our forties with two boys in their teens, we simply did not expect either of our sons to die or be killed. Death of a child, either natural or accidental, was outside the range of expectation. As Dr. Raible said, "It was a bummer."

Yet disaster does strike and accidents do happen. I knew that from my experience as a person and as a pastor. I was well aware of many profound tragedies in our family down through the centuries. We still weren't prepared. I still cannot describe our feelings of shock and loss.

The outpouring of love from family and a wide circle of friends was enormously helpful. This taught me the necessary, even essential lesson that maintaining social contacts and friendships as long as possible is one of life's most important activities.

The Memorial Service, the full text of which is printed here as an appendix, was a key element in pointing me in the fundamental direction of being able to continue to say, "Yes" to life.

Kent's life was a good life, a full life, a useful life, a vital life. He truly said, "Yes" to life. Could I do less? Not really.

It soon dawned on me that I needed to remember him and memorialize him by living the best life of which I was capable, which is what he would have done. Fortunately, Mary shared that belief, fully and completely.

We knew from articles in newspapers and magazines that the death of a child, whether naturally or accidentally, puts an enormous strain on a marriage. The survival rate for such marriages is quite low. Yet we had a satisfying, fulfilling marriage, undergirded by that elusive, hard to define quality called "LOVE," and we wanted to continue our life journey together. We also had a fifteen year old son, David, whom we loved and for whom we felt a deep and basic responsibility.

The most important keys to my ability to move forward with my life are difficult to explain in words, yet vital to an understanding of how life moved along for us.

I have been, and still am to this day, influenced deeply by what is often called "The American Experience." This story has many components, one of the most important of which is "A Spirit of Optimism."

Optimism has fueled my life ever since I can remember. It has served me well and I believe that an understanding of what optimism is and how it affects one's life is enormously important.

Optimism fuels the Creative Imagination. It is far more likely that individuals and nations will survive and come up with solutions to problems and dilemmas if the quest is carried forth in a Spirit of Optimism.

Secondly, Optimism fuels our energy level. Far more Creative Energy is available for any situation if one has optimism, measured and limited though that optimism may be.

Thirdly, Optimism is contagious. Communicated to others sensitively and effectively Optimism produces Creative Cooperation or Creative Interchange so that solutions are found and obstacles are overcome and surmounted.

Coupled with this Spirit of Optimism, and deeply related, is my mother's advice to always let go of the negative emotions of yesterday, which has never left me. About 1964 I came across a brief reading in the Unitarian Universalist hymnal, Hymns for the Celebration of Life. It spoke to me so powerfully that I began a daily morning Quiet Time, beginning with this reading, every morning.

Look to this day!
For it is life, the very life of life.
In its brief course lie all the verities
and realities of your existence:
The bliss of growth,
The glory of action,
The splendor of beauty:
For yesterday is but a dream,
And tomorrow is only a vision;
But today, well lived, makes every
yesterday a dream of happiness
And every tomorrow a vision of Hope.
Look well, therefore, to this day.
—Attributed to Kalidasa

Mary took the view that Kent was such an avid climber that had he not died on Mt. Shuksan he would likely have died on some other mountain.

Although I cannot speak for her, or speculate as to her thoughts, the events of the next weeks, months and years indicate clearly that we decided, individually and as a couple, to get on with life: we would continue to Look to this day!

The best evidence of this is that we had agreed to go on a major trip up the coast on Shenandoah that summer of 1972.

Young friends of ours had a very small sloop, Meander. They had never been to Desolation Sound and we agreed that we would travel together with Shenandoah as the mother-ship.

Hesitantly and quite tentatively and with considerable reluctance and uncertainty, I put the question to Mary, "Shall we go?"

Her immediate response was, "Certainly. They're counting on us, and that's what we promised we would do. We need to get on with life!"

So, three weeks after the memorial service, we went on a most memorable cruise, weeping and laughing and saying "Yes" to Life.

Later that year we set in motion the Kent Hood Evans Endowed Scholarship at Lakeside School.

The road we traveled was surely not easy. Each and every day there is an empty place in our family. This is as true today as it was in 1972. No matter what the occasion, there is and always will be someone missing from the family circle.

There is a reasonable chance that had Kent lived, the close friendship with Bill might have continued and he might possibly have been a co-founder of Microsoft. We obviously don't know any of that because it never happened. I do know, however, without an ounce of doubt, that had he telephoned me from Stanford or Harvard or wherever and said he was taking a leave of absence to join with Bill and Paul in a new venture, I would have said "Go for it!"

His compelling vision was to put a computer on every desk.

(12) RENEWED CONFIDENCE

David graduated from Lakeside School in the Class of 1975 and that fall enrolled at Western Washington University in Bellingham. For the first time, our home was empty of the high energies of young life.

Mary continued with the League of Women Voters and the Council of Planning Affiliates. I worked on various church-related activities, both in the Pacific Northwest District of the Unitarian Universalist Association, and in my national church organizational responsibilities.

I have never investigated the literature on the subject yet it is my experience, individually and as a parish minister, that the grief that follows sudden death of a son, especially accidental death, often has a serious effect on the father's ability to function both personally and professionally.

This was certainly true for me. It seemed that I had overcome the individual part but the professional part was another matter.

Just before we embarked on the summer cruise described in Chapter 14, the Dodge Polara 880 gave up the ghost. It was ten years old and needed a new engine so we let it go. Upon our return we bought a new Peugeot with rack and pinion steering and four-wheel disc brakes. I am not a car enthusiast yet the Peugeot, which we kept for ten years and then replaced with another one, was simply fun to drive. An acquaintance described it as a "thinking person's car."

In 1975-76 we celebrated our 50th birthdays, on December 2 and

January 2. We cleared the large great room of our house and gave a dance party to welcome our forthcoming years.

Early in 1976, to celebrate, honor and participate in the U.S. Bicentennial, we decided to take a 13 week 12,000 mile trip around the United States. Mary, in her wonderfully methodical way of doing things, went to AAA and came home with a huge quantity of maps, Tour Books and Trip Tiks. She was a superb navigator, on land and water, and went at it with thoroughness and attention to detail that always amazed me. She made a tentative plan to visit scenic places, historic sites and museums, former haunts and whatever struck our fancy.

We left home in mid-February, drove south to Bakersfield, CA, and then headed east. We went to Atlanta after which we worked our way slowly up the east coast. We had some definite engagements with relatives and friends of long-standing yet much of the time was flexible.

We visited a cousin of Mary's who lived in West Grove, Pennsylvania. One incident that occurred there was relevant to what happened the following year.

Easter Sunday of 1976 found us at the Sheraton Inn, in Valley Forge, Pennsylvania. We stayed at that particular place, the Sheraton Inn, because as we went along Mary developed her ability to select and locate very nice accommodations.

We attended church services several times along the way but not every Sunday. However, I knew there was a large Unitarian church nearby, in the town of Devon. So, we went to their service. Several years earlier the congregation had purchased an estate with a large fieldstone house. They had added a beautifully proportioned auditorium, also fieldstone, which they called the "Meeting Room."

We were greeted warmly and had an impromptu sandwich lunch with the minister and his spouse in the Dutch-colonial parsonage about a hundred yards from the main building.

When we left, I had a strange, seemingly illogical feeling that somehow, someday, we would return to that lovely place. It clearly appealed to me.

We arrived back home in mid-May. That fall Mary resumed her activities in the League of Women Voters and the Council of Planning Affiliates (COPA), and I continued various church activities, regionally and nationally.

The Council of Planning Affiliates (COPA) was organizing a number of study groups, including a Task Force on Sexual Minorities (TFSM). This was designed to deal with issues and problems facing gay, lesbian, bisexual and transgendered persons. I knew very little about these matters. Just six years earlier, in June of 1970, the Unitarian Universalist General Assembly, meeting in Seattle, had affirmed by General Resolution the validity and appropriateness of Alternate Lifestyles. I knew several close friends who were struggling with these issues so I joined the task force.

It was a life-changing experience. We interviewed many people, experts and ordinary folks, and learned much about a situation that was not yet on the public radar, liberal western Washington included. One prominent public health physician told us that in his opinion a very serious illness was on the horizon. This of course was HIV and AIDS.

Participation on the task force was not easy. Two volunteer chairpersons had to resign because of pressure from their employer even though they worked for social service agencies. Many of the members of the TFSM were participating furtively.

The task force had a United Way staff person assigned to do most of the scheduling and making arrangements for persons to be interviewed.

Once again, a chairperson who was financially and socially invulnerable was needed. Mary and I couldn't be fired from anything and our host of friends at University Unitarian Church would never desert us short of committing a major felony. So I volunteered to chair the taskforce and this role turned into a significant growth experience. I became painfully aware of the plight of persons whose only real agenda was being able to live the lives they were intended to live.

The TFSM produced a report which was immediately buried in a file cabinet at United Way. However, awareness was raised and many of our concerns came to the forefront in later years. It was a very worthwhile effort. To use an ancient yet still useful expression, "Rome was not built in a day." A study group in such a controversial area of human life could not possibly be expected to produce instant results or discernible progress. However, it brought together a large number of people who needed to be in contact with each other which is a more lasting benefit of such groups and one that is often overlooked.

The experience of chairing the task force helped me regain my confidence that I could function at a reasonably high level of proficiency.

Meanwhile I maintained my contacts with the Department of Ministry at the UUA. Congregations all across the country, Unitarian and otherwise, were discovering that when long time pastors retired or died, and were succeeded by someone else, the new settlements had a very high rate of failure. There needed to be a more intentional interim period, with more professional leadership than was typical of the rather lackadaisical approach that had been in place for centuries.

The Alban Institute, a resource and consulting resource for pastors and congregations, located in Washington, D.C, had designed a program for full-time, full-salary transition staff, called Accredited Interim Ministry, or AIM. The purpose of AIM was to enable a congregation to make a successful transition, and become much stronger and more vital while making that significant change.

Mary and I decided that such a program appealed to us so I applied for and was admitted to the first group of UU ministers who were to receive the training. Various UU ministers had been doing forms of interim ministry for a number of years but this group of six was to receive training, using the Alban Institute model.

Our particular training was under the auspices of the New Hampshire-Vermont Conference of the United Church of Christ, and took place in Concord, New Hampshire. I flew to Boston and we went to Concord as a group. At the conclusion of the course I received a certificate as an Accredited Interim Minister.

The UUA staff person in charge, Dr. David Pohl, took us to a restaurant on Beacon Street and reviewed the possible placements for September.

UU congregations are totally independent of any higher control and they were in no mood to participate in a very expensive program that would delay the calling of a new settled minister for one or two years. The failure rate was overshadowed by other concerns, mainly money.

The other five members of our group needed jobs and needed them badly, so Dr. Pohl and I agreed that I would hold back until the others were placed. I would be in reserve.

However, I knew that the Main Line Unitarian Church (MLUC) in Devon had lost its first and only minister so when Dr. Pohl finished his list I inquired about Devon. He said that Devon decided against an interim, in spite of his entreaties, and expected to call a new minister who would assume the pastorate in September.

I must have rolled my eyes (Dr. Pohl confirmed this later) but I just remarked that if the situation should change I would appreciate being kept in mind because I would love to go there.

I returned home and Mary and I made plans to go up the coast aboard Shenandoah for the summer. One night we were in my study chatting when the telephone rang and Mary answered. She cupped the phone and said, "It's Devon."

It was two members of the Board of Trustees at MLUC. The minister had taken a new position quite early in the year. He was an excellent pastor yet by his own admission he ran the operation as his personal enterprise, in a style I call "out of his inside coat pocket."

It was obvious they weren't going to have a new minister by September and they had at long last decided they needed an AIM. Dr. Pohl had given them my name, with a high recommendation, that I very much appreciated.

I flew east for an interview. We came to a satisfactory agreement yet it was quite limited in duration so we held to our plans to go cruising and told them we would drive across the continent and hope to arrive there in mid-September, about a month later than we would have gone if the agreement had not been so limited.

We did just that. We had a delightful summer and arrived in Devon in mid-September. They insisted that we live in the lovely parsonage which they had furnished very nicely.

It turned out that much essential planning and arranging of the life of the congregation had not been done. They were busy, highly educated professional people with limited discretionary time but most importantly, no one was in charge of the store. No "chief of operations" was on duty, day in and day out, making sure things got done. It was a MESS!

What saved me was that I went there with six sermons and six Orders of Worship completed and ready. They were still of many minds as to whether they needed or even wanted an AIM. I found myself looking for opportunities to get their attention.

Finally, my chance came by way of classic serendipity.

Mary Sohier, the chair of our Music Committee, was doing the one-person play, The Belle of Amherst, based on the life of Emily Dickinson, at a local Little Theatre. Mary and I simply hadn't found time to attend. Finally it was closing night, Saturday night. This was the last opportunity – do or die. Mary had a terrible cold so she suggested I go alone, which I did.

During the long intermission, needed because it is a solo performance, I went downstairs and proceeded to serve myself from a large assortment of quite elegant pastries, plus coffee. As I began to enjoy my goodies, I was approached by eight parishioners, in a group. They had gone to dinner and were attending the play together.

One of them, best described as an "in your face" type, blurted out, without any greeting, "What are YOU doing HERE?"

I'd experienced one or two encounters with him (he led the charge against having an AIM) and was determined to not be bested so I replied.

"Well, Mary Sohier is doing The Belle of Amherst, and it's closing night. I am here to see the performance, which I am enjoying very much."

This obviously fueled the battle of two very strong wits.

"Well, Mason [the given name of the previous pastor] NEVER went ANYWHERE on Saturday night"

"I'm sorry, Bob, but my name is Marvin, not Mason, and it is against my religion to work on Saturday night, unless I have a wedding."

At that point the others joined in and regaled me with marvelous tales of the Saturday habits of Mason, and his wife, Dorothy, including Dorothy prancing around the parsonage muttering, "I hate Saturday. I hate Saturday."

When I returned home, Mary was awake and I told her what had happened.

"That explains everything! I have been hearing about all these Saturday events, and we haven't been invited to anything. I was beginning to worry. They all think you work on Saturday!"

The next morning, at services during the Announcements period, I stepped out of the pulpit and off the chancel and told what had happened. Then I said, "So, if any of you would enjoy our company on Saturday, invite us and in all likelihood we will accept."

From then on, they understood what interim ministry was all about. We're all different and they needed to decide what and whom they wanted next.

The year went well, although they contended, correctly, that I was quite rough with them.

They deserved to have someone be rough, tough and fearless with them. I relished the role! Their organizational structure was suitable for a congregation one-fourth their size, and their finances were in shambles.

This is also where I discovered the Evans Parking Lot Test, which has served me so well for more than thirty years. It works like this:

If you want a quick, easy, simple almost fool-proof assessment of any organization, public or private, profit or non-profit, and that organization has a parking lot or a parking garage, take a careful stroll through that facility and look at the vehicles being driven by the members or customers or patrons of that organization. It will tell you almost instantly what you have or don't have, as the case may be. Almost everyone at MLUC came by car and the lot was filled with Mercedes, BMW and other expensive cars. Yet the salaries they paid to their staff were disgraceful, while they pleaded poverty. I shamed them into doing better. I did it and I was glad.

Devon is located in the Brandywine Valley and it is a truly beautiful area. Mary's relatives on the Hood side of her family settled there about 1750, and her grandfather, W.T. Hood, was born there. We had a great time visiting graves and other sites connected with her family. We covered many miles of back roads in the Peugeot. The Chester County Historical Society had a series of audiotapes, and Mary did extensive family research in the court records, located in West Chester.

All in all it was one of the best years of our 51 years together. My professional confidence was restored and raised to an even higher level. I still knew how to be a minister.

The MLUC congregation called a new minister, so we had to decide what to do next. Once again, serendipity served us well.

* * *

The Unitarian Universalist Association and the separate UU Ministers Association had established a joint endeavor called the Office of Ministerial Finances, located in Eliot House, one of the auxiliary buildings of the headquarters complex on Beacon Hill. It was at best a hybrid concept, designed to consolidate a variety of programs in the areas of group insurance, pensions, emergency financial assistance and advocacy for improved salaries, benefits and allowances for ministers.

There had never been a consolidated, systematic approach to these important and complex matters during the 150 years since the American Unitarian Association was founded in 1825.

Gaining traction is always difficult in such a situation and the person appointed to be the Director of Ministerial Finances was terminated. Thus the parties to the situation were seeking an Interim Director while they decided what to do next. There was an undercurrent that the UUA wanted to terminate the effort.

I had virtually no technical knowledge of the complex matters involved, yet once again what was needed was a fearless, independent person who had no career ambitions and would help them sort it all out, without fear or favor. I had served on the Board of Trustees of the UUA and had been in and out of Boston many times. I knew full well that UUA Headquarters is a classic example of a mini-bureaucracy, staffed with highly educated people who have difficulty deciding anything. Decision-making time is a direct function of education level, the more education people have, the longer it takes to decide anything.

A dear friend of mine was overseeing all this and asked me to come to Boston and look at the situation. I went with a considerable degree of healthy skepticism.

The appointment was to be for one year. Mary and I had never lived in the inner city as a couple. The idea of a year in downtown Boston appealed to us, so we accepted the appointment.

I always left the choice of apartments and houses to Mary. She found a very nice apartment on the 31st floor of a new building at One Longfellow Place, in Charles River Park. This was within easy walking distance of Eliot House, where my office would be located. The apartment had a wonderful view to seaward and if you stepped out on the small balcony you could see the U.S.S. Constitution, "Old Ironsides."

We spent the summer in Seattle and returned to Boston in the fall.

I could easily write a separate memoir about this adventure. Suffice it to say that the job was incredibly complicated and complex, and far more difficult than I ever envisioned. Accomplishing forward movement and progress is extremely difficult in a mini-bureaucracy, public or private, profit or non-profit.

Perhaps the most valuable, long lasting lessons I learned is that small committees and boards ought to function by consensus, not votes, and that defined-benefit pension plans are untenable by definition. No one, and I mean absolutely no one, can design a defined benefit plan that will be sustainable over the long haul, and this is why so many of these plans have either collapsed or are in serious trouble in 2009. Fortunately, the plan available to ministers and other church staff is a defined contribution plan.

Mary and I enjoyed life in downtown Boston but missed our house in Seattle, missed Shenandoah, which we left in the care of a friend, and most of all, missed the freedom of being able to arrange our schedule in ways that suited us and our interests. We also missed University Unitarian Church of Seattle and our many friends there.

During our all too brief time aboard Shenandoah that summer, we decided that operating a sailboat and having to be outside in both rain and sunshine was no longer our understanding of fun. Mary read a story in which the woman of a man-woman sailing couple insisted on asking, quite frequently, 'Is this fun?' If the answer was, 'No,' then she insisted on changing course and doing something else that was fun such as putting into a nice harbor and finding the nearest bar or restaurant.

We didn't want a power boat so we decided to look for a pilot house sailboat. Not a motor sailer but a full-rig sailing vessel with a proper wheel house, equipped with inside steering so it could be sailed from the inside, out of the weather.

After an exhaustive search in the United States and Canada, we found a small company in New Hampshire that agreed to build what we wanted. Mary spent much of the winter laying out the interior of her boat, while I wrote the mechanical specifications. She did a wonderful job. It was the best laid-out boat of its kind I have ever seen. It had her fingerprints all over it. She also designed her own ship's log book and had it custom printed to her specifications. Brandywine, named for that lovely river and valley in southeastern Pennsylvania, was completed in the late spring of 1980 and shipped to Seattle on a flat bed truck.

The commissioning of Brandywine made our situation in Boston even more untenable, so I resigned my position (I had been given a permanent appointment in 1979) and returned to Seattle, never to leave again for any extended length of time.

Taken in full and on balance, our three years in Boston constituted a very good experience for us. Notwithstanding the never-ceasing noise and the ever-present brightness of the lights of the inner city, we really and truly enjoyed apartment living and enjoyed being downtown. This set the stage for our permanent move to downtown Seattle in 1993.

(13) THE EXCITING EIGHTIES

On our way back from Boston to Seattle, we stopped in Ottawa, Canada for several days. An ancestor of Mary's had a sister who married Thomas McKay and they settled in Ottawa. McKay was an early prominent citizen of Ottawa and headed a company that constructed early sections of the Rideau Canal. The Ottawa Historical Society had recently mounted a major exhibit on McKay. The exhibit had been dismantled yet we were able to see and read some of the panels.

It was good to be home. We resumed many of our volunteer interests in Seattle and about 1979 I took a seat on the Board of Trustees of Meadville Theological School, where I had received my degree in 1963. My term continued until 1983.

Meanwhile, the Unitarian Universalist Association was trying to increase the level of financial support provided to them by individual congregations, which were autonomous. They set a recommended contribution amount, per member, and congregations that met that level were designated Honor Societies. Funding for the Pacific Northwest District (PNWD) followed the same formula.

There were more than fifty congregations in the Pacific Northwest District and Mary was asked to take charge of the fundraising effort. She took the title of Chair of the Annual Program Fund but in actuality we took the portfolio together.

Mary set out to secure as many Honor Societies as possible, a formidable task indeed. Figuratively speaking, the only way to go was

UP. We bought an IBM PC Jr. computer and set up a database with an early program called Filing Assistant. We knew intuitively that the only way to increase the number of Honor Societies was to help the congregations improve their local fund-raising because the two items we were promoting were line items in their operating budget.

So, I wrote and circulated two handbooks on local church fund-raising and we offered free workshops throughout the PNWD. After several years I took the title as Chair. We did this together until late in the decade when we decided, wisely, that people were getting tired of being hounded for money by us and the program needed new ideas and new leadership. The success was sustained until the present economic downturn when many congregations are experiencing serious financial pressure. I have the feeling it will take many years to reestablish the program to full strength.

Meanwhile, serendipity appeared once again. The Bellingham Unitarian Fellowship, in the lovely coastal city of that name, north of Seattle, had limped along for many years but was growing substantially. They had a love-hate relationship with a few ministers but had been essentially lay-led for many years. They had a small frame church building with an adjoining parsonage which they had purchased many years earlier. They had long ago ceased to have a church office or any paid staff. The church telephone was in the basement recreation room of one of the dedicated members. They had contracted with a nearby minister for a very part-time program called Consulting Ministry, beginning in September of 1984. That person was unable to take the job, and no one else seemed to be available.

Once again, the phone at 1515 N.W. Woodbine Way rang. It was Rod Stewart, District Executive, asking if I was interested in coming out of retirement, again, and taking the job in Bellingham.

"Thanks, but No Thanks. I'm retired. Finished. Out of here. Gone. Take my name off the list, now and forevermore."

Rod and I had worked together over the years on many sticky wickets and we understood each other.

"Well, would you go up there and look at it, give me your assessment, and any suggestions as to someone who might be able to work with them? They're schizophrenic. They want a minister who isn't a real minister."

"That's NOT me."

"I know, but would you just go and look at it. I am really in a hole."

"Sure, I'll go up there. They'll be sorry they ever saw me, but that's their problem, not mine."

"Great. I'll have one of their people contact you."

We made arrangements for me to lead a worship service and then meet with their Board of Trustees over an informal lunch.

What I found was absolutely fascinating. The small sanctuary, located upstairs, as was typical of these early 20th century church buildings, was jam-packed to overflowing. A fire marshal's nightmare. The open-ended Announcements period, during which anyone could announce anything, seemed as though it would never end. When we finally reached the sermon, which seemed like an insert designed to satisfy a few minister lovers. I had seven minutes before the end of the hour. So, I gave a short talk and the service ended.

However, what I also found was a large number of well-educated, well-motivated people, eager and anxious to get on with the show.

After a brutally frank discussion of my intention to move then to a very different level, they offered me the position of Consulting Minister and I accepted.

In the short space of two years, with me essentially as their coach, they purchased a much more adequate building, established a staffed office, engaged a full-time minister and other staff as needed. More than twenty years later they are thriving and are now expanding their facilities by adding a new building on the same site.

It was my final ministerial post and a very satisfying project. They received permission from UUA Headquarters to call me to the permanent designation of Minister Emeritus, which, among other things, gives me full delegate credentials at the annual General Assembly. This is one of my most cherished and prized designations. It is not automatic. It must be earned and I feel that although my

ministerial career was atypical, I made some had some major contributions I helped two congregations − Victoria, B.C. and Bellingham, WA, reach what I call orbit, and both are still in orbit.

Also, the congregation in Devon made a successful transition and
the UUA Office of Church Staff Finances is flourishing.

Because I did not have a job in the conventional sense, I was frequently asked to do special assignments, often ones that would
have involved substantial risk for ministers who were trying to
pursue a career with some measure of success and fulfillment.

For example, if a minister and a congregation are having problems
and difficulties, it is frequently helpful to send in a resource person
who is totally independent, not beholden to anything or anybody.
Speaking individually and not sociologically, I found this role to
be very stimulating, exciting and fulfilling. I could just go in, take
a very careful look at the situation, listen attentively, and then describe the situation as I perceived it, without fear or favor.

Gradually, over a period of twenty years, I developed the ability,
perhaps the talent, to differentiate between what I personally like or
prefer, and what the situation needs and requires. Very frequently,
those two aspects of any situation are quite different.

The fundamental dilemma is associated with every organization,
public or private, profit or non-profit, even the basic unit of the
family.

There is another stark reality, namely the inability to differentiate
between what I hope will happen, or want to have happen, on the
one hand, and what is highly likely to happen, on the other hand.
Again, these may not be one and the same.

It seems to me that these two lessons, combined with an ability and
willingness to let go of the negative emotions of yesterday, are basic to what I call "The Religious Quest." They are essential elements
of any serious effort to attain peace, contentment and fulfillment.

I call this "Standing Back" This means standing back from the pres-
sures and demands of the moment and asking myself and others
"What's this all about?"

My primary frame of reference is found in the Seven Principles of the Unitarian Universalist Association of Congregations, adopted over a period of years by General Assemblies of the organization.

- The inherent worth and dignity of every person

- Justice, equity and compassion in human relations

- Acceptance of one another and encouragement to spiritual growth in our congregations

- A free and responsible search for truth and meaning

- the right of conscience and the use of the democratic process in our congregations and in society at large

- The goal of world community with peace, liberty and justice for all

- Respect for the interdependent web of all existence of which we are a part.

The Living Tradition we share draws from Six Sources:

- Direct experience of that transcending mystery and wonder, affirmed in all cultures, which moves us to a renewal of the spirit and an openness to the forces which create and uphold life;

- Words and deeds of prophetic women and men which challenge us to confront powers and structures of evil with justice, compassion, and the transforming power of love;

- Wisdom from the world's religions, which inspires us in our ethical and spiritual life;

- Jewish and Christian teachings which call us to respond to God's love by loving our neighbors as ourselves;

- Humanist teachings, which counsel us to heed the guidance of reason and the results of science, and warn us against idolatries of the mind and spirit;

- Spiritual teachings of earth-centered traditions, which celebrate the sacred circle of life and instruct us to live in harmony with the rhythms of nature.

From the standpoint of the choices and decisions I make each and every day, the most difficult of the Seven Principles, by far, is the Second Principle: justice, equity and compassion in human relations.

Not so much for someone out there in a distant foreign land, but rather here, now, today, in my daily life. I must strive to implement this principle with everyone with whom I interact, day in and day out, and, most especially, I must begin with myself.

There is a short piece that I keep on the end table in my living room, right beside where I sit to read and watch television. Living alone as I do, it is my principal perching place. It was written many years ago by The Reverend Vilma Szantho Harrington.

Causes, Yes; People, No!

Give me causes, Oh God, to theorize,
argue, talk about. Let me think of problems far away.
Let me go to luncheons, dinners,
for tired celebrities, with long speeches,
speeches about causes.
Let me raise money, money to support
big offices with large staffs
to do a little good for someone,
someone far away.
Give me causes, Oh God,
Causes to forget the miseries that are too close
to hide, but don't, Oh God, don't let me be
involved with people. People are too near.
People may enter my home, may cry before my eyes.
People can be hungry, ragged, even dirty.
They may ask me to give - to give without publicity.
People may be rude.
They may ask me to identify with them
intimately, when all I want is not to be involved.
I want to be interested, God, yes interested.
Causes help me to be interested.
And informed. People get me involved.
Do give me causes, Oh God, to theorize,
argue, talk about. Let me think
of problems far away.

Day in and day out, no matter what I am doing or with whom I am involved, I try to pose a number of questions so as to test my grasp of the situation and frame my response.

First Question: In this specific situation, right here and now, have I really and truly, Let go of yesterday? All too frequently, a candid, frank answer simply must be "No."

Second Question: Am I adequately attuned to the Second Principle? Justice, equity and compassion in human relations.

Third Question: Am I differentiating between what I prefer and what the situation requires, and am I attuned to the difference between what I want to have happen and what is likely to happen?

Fourth Question: If the matter at hand is an issue related to public policy, such as universal health care, death with dignity, human rights, and a host of other issues, Will my attitude, my response, my decision(s) put me On the Right Side of History? I would submit that if you look carefully at the history of what is now the United States of America, since the first permanent English settlement at James Towne, Virginia, in 1607, the movement, the journey, the pathway has clearly been in the direction of the Second Principle. The pathway has certainly not been what I would call straightline, yet we are, as a society, clearly more just and equitable and compassionate than we were four hundred years ago.

The Fifth, and Final Question: In this particular situation, no matter how mundane or how major, am I really and truly saying, "Yes" to Life?

I have written all this, in this particular chapter, for a very specific and compelling reason:

My personal, individual understanding of who I am and what my life is all about didn't really take shape and gain real meaning and real traction until the decade when I was between the ages of 55 and 65. From that point until now, life has been exciting and difficult and incredibly rich and interesting.

* * *

One other very important development needs to be mentioned before we move along with the story.

Sometime about 1988, we aren't exactly certain as to the date, my friend and ministerial colleague, Bill Houff, and I began keeping personal journals and exchanged them weekly with each other by regular mail. We maintained them originally by typewriter and later by word processing. Once a week we produce a hard copy, by whatever means, and simply put it in the mail. No electronic mail and no electronic attachments.

The journal is often accompanied by half a dozen inserts, such as Orders of Worship, newspaper and magazine articles and other items of interest. We read different publications, thus the clippings broaden our range of knowledge and information. We are still doing this after twenty years, and it enriches my life beyond description. I have never been able to identify any other two people, men or women, who have done this for twenty years.

Journal-keeping is an ancient practice. For me, it has several important aspects. I am an intense person. I find it very helpful to supplement my daily "Quiet Time" with a daily "Journal Time." I can reflect on the events of the day and frequently let go of the negative emotions of "yesterday" before yesterday even arrives.

Secondly, our exchange has resulted in a relationship that is deep; thus when a crisis arises we are present to each other and for each other at a deep level. We can often affect and change for the better the clouded emotional reading one frequently experiences in the midst of crisis. Sometimes this means picking up the phone and talking the matter through to reach a more helpful stance.

(14) CRUISING IN PARADISE

A dominant motif in my family for at least four centuries has been tidal salt water. I frequently say that I have it in my veins. The particular bodies of water which have had such a marked effect on us and define our story are the Chesapeake Bay and its many tributaries, the Atlantic Ocean from Savannah, Georgia to Halifax, Nova Scotia, and the inland waters of Washington and British Columbia from Seattle to Campbell River.

My earliest memories include Norfolk Harbor, the Elizabeth River, which flows through both Brambleton and Chesterfield Heights, Chesapeake Bay and the shores of Pungoteague Creek and Occahannock Creek on Virginia's Eastern Shore. These places were where I became a "wharf rat."

The term has no polite equivalent. A "wharf rat" is someone whose natural, preferred, necessary, essential habitat is a pier, a float, a dock, a wharf of any description. We are at our happiest, most contented selves when we are ensconced in such a place. We can be there indefinitely, doing nothing.

After eighteen years of such an existence, I essentially experienced twenty years as an "inlander." It was not the right place for me. Fortunately during most of that time my mother still lived in Norfolk which gave me good reason to visit her and smell the salt water. Virginia Beach continued to be a favorite place as it had been during my high school years.

All of this changed dramatically when we moved to Oak Bay, British Columbia in 1963. As related earlier, our house was just a short distance from Oak Bay and the Oak Bay Marina.

I date my figurative rebirth from the time we took delivery of the first Shalom, a CAL 20, in May of 1964. It was, and still is, a wonderful boat. David and I saw a refurbished one several years ago and it took our breath away. It was simply beautiful. It was also forgiving in the sense that it was gentle with novice keel-boat sailors like me, and kept me out of trouble. Because we intended to cruise as a family, we also bought a small plywood dinghy or pram.

David and Kent learned to row the pram. David has vivid memories of the boat being tied to the dock with a rope so he could not roam very far. Kent was 9 and David was 7. These were formative years for both of them, and they learned about independence and self-reliance, and attention to detail.

There are no log books from those days yet we have fond memories of rowing and sailing and what is called gunk-holing. The word is not even contained in my online dictionary; a disgraceful omission.

Katie Hafner, writing in the August 8, 1993 (our 40th wedding anniversary) issue of The New York Times describes the ancient and honorable term beautifully.

> "Off the coast of Washington and British Columbia, tucked away like so many hidden jewels, are the San Juan and Gulf Islands, at once civilized and untrampled. To explore them in a way that was free of structure... we chartered a sailboat and set out for a week of gunk-holing.

> "Gunk-holing is a kind of nautical meandering dipping in and out of coves and inlets. The San Juans and their sister archipelago to the north, the Gulfs, turned out to be an ideal place to do it."

Mary, Kent and David had never sailed. I had never owned a boat that size with a fixed keel, so we began with day sails near the marina, one of the most beautiful spots imaginable. Mt. Baker, Washington, dominates the skyline to the east.

The CAL 20 had a tiny cabin with four sleeping spaces and a toilet (a "head" in nautical language) but no permanent cooking facilities (or galley) and no standing head room. It had a large cockpit so a local company made a large boom tent that could enclose the entire cockpit at night or in bad weather. We called it the mausoleum. We were truly camping.

Gradually and carefully we ventured farther from our leased dock at the Oak Bay Marina. The possibilities were almost endless.

I tried the Wednesday night races at the Royal Victoria Yacht Club but racing is simply not in my genes.

We had summers of freedom to sail and explore since most Unitarian churches in that day and age closed after the second Sunday in June and remained closed until the second Sunday in September.

Although Mary loved being on the boat, especially as a family, she never in her entire life learned the first thing about the art and practice of sailing and operating a boat. Rather, it was her summer home, and she was quite content to live aboard for weeks at a time without ever sleeping ashore or going to her other home. I distinctly recall one cruise of fifty-four days. Friends and acquaintances were amazed that the four of us spent that length of time living in what amounted to a floating tent.

The international border between the United States and Canada is not far from Oak Bay. Roche Harbor, Washington, soon became one of our favorite places. Located on the northwest corner of San Juan Island, it had been in the 19th and early 20th centuries a large lime-producing operation, one of the largest on the west coast. In addition to the lime producing plant it had (and still has) a hotel, a general store, a large dining room in what was originally the family home, a swimming pool and many other amenities. It has been enlarged in recent years and is one of the outstanding marine resorts in Washington and British Columbia.

David and Kent could beach comb and gunk-hole and swim and be wharf rats, always with lots of companions of their own ages. Mary specialized in reading aboard the boat and in having delicious meals ashore. In addition, hundreds of pleasure boats of every type, size and description came to the harbor to make use of the seasonal office of the U.S. Customs and Immigration Service. Because the two countries are so closely linked, clearing customs was a frequent, ever-present activity.

Rowing the pram dinghy had its limits, for the boys and especially for father, so we bought a small, unique Evinrude 3hp outboard motor that had a hinged shaft so that it folded in half and was easy to carry and stow. The boys loved it. It was in a very real sense their first motor vehicle. Obviously small outboard engines can be swung around and maneuvered and David learned the art of that. Later he could do things with the larger boats that I wouldn't dream of even attempting to do. He developed a very useful lifetime skill. What he can do with a boat is nothing short of amazing.

It was during these years that both Kent and David developed a deep love and deep respect for tidal salt water. For rocks and reefs, for tides and currents, for depths and shallows, for wind and human frailty in a marine environment. David is still a "wharf rat" and natural sailor.

During the summer of 1968 I was on duty part of the time at University Unitarian Church of Seattle, so we kept the boat at Rosario Resort on Orcas Island. The family lived aboard while I commuted back and forth to our other home in Seattle.

Memory is simply unclear as to what year we first went north (into Canada), as we did many times during the next thirty years. It is probable that we did so as early as 1967, the summer we lived aboard while transitioning from Victoria to Seattle. Going North is a different order of magnitude. Many veteran pleasure boat enthusiasts never cross the Strait of Georgia to the Sunshine Coast of British Columbia. Although it is part of the Inside Passage, it is about seventeen miles across and one needs to know what one is doing. Wind and tide, especially when moving in opposite directions, can create conditions that require a good measure of knowledge and seamanship. Many people learn that the hard way.

There are thousands of descriptions of what one finds on the mainland coast. I have perhaps read hundreds of them but never one that even began to tell the story. It is simply a different world from the settings to which most of us are accustomed.

Continuing up the Sunshine Coast, one comes to the famous idyllic area that Captain George Vancouver named Desolation Sound.

This area became a favorite destination of ours for many years to come.

The main road ends at Bliss Landing, just north of the village of Lund, British Columbia. The tidal currents divide around Vancouver Island and meet in the Desolation Sound area, thus the water is warm enough that one can swim comfortably. Although there are a few scattered residents the entire area is essentially uninhabited.

One account I can locate is a short theme written by Kent for Lit. 7-1 at Lakeside. It is brief yet it sets the stage for what became a very important formative place for Kent and David, and for the Evans family. None of us has been there since 1996 yet both the influences and the memories are quite strong and significant.

Kent's piece is titled simply "Mink Island."

> "This summer we cruised on our sailboat for six weeks in the San Juans, the Gulf Islands, on the Sunshine Coast and in Desolation Sound.

> "Mink Island, called Repulse Island on some American charts, is one of the best places we visited. It is in Desolation Sound and is about two hundred miles north of Seattle.

> "The island is about two miles long. On the south side of the island there is a little cove behind a small island which protects it from the wind. Anchorage in the cove is good. Refuge Cove, which has a fuel dock, moorage, ice and a good store, is just half an hour away ... under power.

> "Swimming is the main attraction of Mink Island. The water is warm and clear. Unfortunately, the shore is rocky and has oyster shells on it in places. The cove is quiet and part of the time we were the only boat anchored there. There are some places along the shore where the water is quite deep and you can dive from the shore.

> "We could only stay for two nights at Mink Island, because we were coming to the end of our holiday and needed to get to Seattle."

We returned to Mink Island many times. It was a truly idyllic place for two young brothers. They could hike and swim and row and beach comb and simply be in contact with themselves and the natural world in a very safe environment.

One summer they found a large, dilapidated wooden hatch cover, probably from a derelict fishing boat. They decided to build a lean-to on the small island. They had only a Swiss Army knife with a saw blade, what Oak Bay Hardware called a "ladies tack hammer" and a bag of large galvanized nails which had somehow found their way aboard the boat. Never mind! They got the job done, and delighted in the results. The next year the lean-to was still there so they dismantled it and turned it into a raft.

Meanwhile, Mary and I could read and swim and stroll on the beach and especially enjoy the sunrises, the sunsets, and the fabulous night skies, far distant from any major city. Mt. Denman dominated the skyline to the east.

Although I enjoyed the two CAL boats, small one person day sailers have always been my first love. After we moved to Seattle we bought a classic small fiberglass dinghy called a Minto, named for the steamboat Lady Minto that plied the waters of Kootenay Lake in British Columbia. Hundreds of them were turned out by various builders. Ours came from the Ranger Boat Company. It sailed beautifully and rowed even more beautifully. The Minto and I formed a deep and lasting bond with each other.

Now, more than forty years later, David still has that love for small day sailers and is teaching young people how to sail them, down in Arizona. He has an affinity learned at a very young age and knows how to relate to youngsters who are just learning the magic of small boat sailing. It is far and away the best time in life to start.

After I gave up the quarter-time position at University Unitarian Church, on May 30, 1969, from then on our summer months were essentially free and unencumbered.

During that same summer, 1969, we explored the waters adjacent to Desolation Sound, between there and Vancouver Island to the west. Between Cortes and Read islands we discovered a small island with a prominent hill called Hill Island in Sutil Channel.

At that time Hill Island was privately owned by Charles H. "Chuck" and Hazel Mitchell, who lived there permanently. They had a lovely house (actually a manufactured home which they enclosed with framing), a lounge-type building with a huge fireplace which they called the Chart Room, three small cabins available to guests, a fuel dock, and a very small, inadequately protected marina with space for probably ten or twelve boats, depending on their size. Outside the Chart Room was a large wooden deck with lounge chairs and chaise lounges and a classic hammock swung between trees.

Chuck Mitchell had developed the island and constructed everything on it with virtually no assistance. He purchased pre-cut buildings and figured out how to erect them, using ingenious yet often simple rigs and devices.

The Mitchell's were very gracious to us and we to them. Hill Island became a very favorite place until they sold the island a few years later.

Here again it was an ideal place for our family. Chuck had a trash-disposal place on the side of the island away from the house. Trash was transported in a small trailer pulled by a small motor scooter. David was in charge of the trash detail, which he absolutely loved. Chuck was a fair yet demanding taskmaster and our explorer David learned that sometimes it was a good idea to do things the way they needed to be done. "Do it right, the first time."

These early years of cruising led Mary and me to the conclusion that we had truly found a way of life that suited us, and that we wanted and needed a larger more comfortable boat which would be our home afloat. We wanted standing head room, proper berths, a galley, a shower and other comforts of home.

The story is perhaps apocryphal yet Mary enjoyed saying that when she sat down in the frying pan, forgetting that she had set it on a bunk, she decided it was time for a larger boat.

We were in our mid-forties, the boys were 14 and 12, we had no mortgage or debts and if we shopped carefully and kept our desires in focus we could purchase a boat without seeking a loan.

Although I provided a good measure of technical advice, I always let Mary take the lead in selecting the houses and the boats. She was quite unusual in the fact that she enjoyed and even cherished long periods aboard, even on very small boats. She had excellent judgment so that if the boat worked for her it would work for us.

After exploring the market, looking at boats new and used, we ordered a Pearson 35 from Pearson Yachts in Rhode Island and had it shipped to Seattle on a flatbed truck. Mary named it Shenandoah for the beautiful river and valley in Virginia. The boat was commissioned in April of 1970 and was a U.S. Coast Guard Documented Vessel, duly listed in Merchant Vessels of the United States, Including Yachts.

It was aboard Shenandoah that David and Kent became expert sailors on a large keel boat. They learned how to rig and reef and trim, how to watch the wind and tide and current, how to steer and how to set an anchor and how to dock and undock in problematic situations. Shenandoah was equipped with Edson pedestal steering so they learned the art of maneuvering a large engine powered craft under both sail and power. And they learned how to get everything shipshape when entering or leaving a harbor or an anchorage. A place for everything, and everything in its place. This is of crucial importance on a boat.

Our first major cruise began on June 7, 1970, and lasted 72 days. On June 17, Kent's closest friend, Bill Gates, Jr., came aboard, and the next day our friend, Jim Munro, owner of Munro's Books in Victoria, B.C. came aboard. We started north and on June 23rd we reached Princess Louisa Inlet. This is one of the most beautiful places on the southwest British Columbia coast. The fjord is perhaps fifty miles long and is ringed with mountains of 8,000 ft. elevation that rise from water that is 2,000 feet deep. Bill and Jim left the vessel at Secret Cove on June 26 and returned to their homes.

Many years later I asked Jim if he remembered that Kent had a friend aboard. He replied, "Yes. I remember a tow-headed kid; they talked computers all the time."

I replied, "That kid was Bill Gates, co-founder of Microsoft." Jim was surprised and amazed. He searched through his photos and found the one included here on p. 99, of the five of us standing in the cockpit. He placed it on the desk in his office at the lovely bookstore, commemorating the summer he went cruising with Bill Gates. It is a great conversation piece.

That summer of 1970 was typical of the longer cruises. We stayed north until August 27 and arrived back at our berth at the Shilshole Bay Marina, Port of Seattle, on September 7.

In January of 1972, at the Seattle Boat Show, we purchased a 16.5 foot runabout manufactured by the Winner Boat Company, of Dickson, Tennessee.

Winner was an early builder of fiberglass boats, and quickly established a reputation for building safe, comfortable attractive boats.

The boat was a vivid yellow. It never really had a name. We always referred to as simply The Winner.

David quickly became Skipper – Captain David! The first few summers we took it north with us. He would skipper it or we would tow it behind Shenandoah, or we towed it by trailer to a convenient spot up the coast.

The Winner made a big difference in our cruising. It vastly increased our range for sightseeing and gunk-holing while at anchor or in port. Resupplying the ship was far easier. The young people water skied for hours on end. Blayney Scott's father, known affectionately to all of us as "Papa," then about 80, even tried his hand at skiing.

David developed more of his instincts for boating while skippering this relatively small boat. He developed a deep respect and appreciation for the power of the sea. Like so many others who love the ships and the sea, he applies his sailing acumen to other parts of his life.

He is truly an Evans, following in the tradition of more than three centuries of "watermen" who have borne that name.

Following Kent's death, we carried a paid crew for many years. Shenandoah did not have a self-furling head sail, self-tailing winches or an autopilot, all of which make single hand sailing much easier. In addition it had an old-style large mainsail which was hard to furl.

By the end of our 1979 cruise, we had taken a total of nine cruises, ranging in length from 29 days to 79 days – a total of 444 days. We knew that cruising the Inside Passage was a major activity for us.

Then we had Brandywine built in New Hampshire and trucked to Seattle, where she awaited us.

Over the next fifteen years we took thirteen cruises, ranging in length from 27 days to 87 days, all of them in the area between Seattle and Desolation Sound, for a total of 656 days.

There was an ever-present temptation to continue farther north than Desolation Sound, to the Broughton Group for example. Mary had an understandable reluctance to do that and, in my judgment doing so required a radar system, which we did not have. So, we essentially never went beyond the general area called Desolation Sound.

If you add together the two experiences, with Shenandoah and Brandywine, there were 22 cruises for a total of 1,100 days, plus the six years on the two boats named Shalom. There were literally hundreds of pleasant, enjoyable, relaxing and yes, memorable experiences.

While writing this chapter I read the two log books thoroughly. We had lovely sails, entertained many friends and relatives and cruised with other boats. We celebrated anniversaries and birthdays and holidays. We had very few problems considering the amount of time we spent aboard.

Cruising and vacationing are two quite different states of being. Usually for the first ten to fourteen days, we were vacationing. Then, almost imperceptibly, the mood would change and life on the vessel would settle down. We shifted from vacationing to living aboard. I am frequently asked, especially by men how we managed to stay aboard for such long periods. I am not sure of the answer(s) to that but two factors probably contributed to the situation. First, all four of the boats were our boats, selected jointly, owned jointly and outfitted jointly. Secondly, I almost always let Mary set the agenda as to where we went and what we did. She liked a leisurely pace, frequently staying a week or more in one place, and preferred to be tied up a dock rather than being on anchor. Yet she knew I loved anchoring in places such as Prideau Haven, and we went there frequently.

We learned to accommodate each other's needs and wishes and desires and to give each other space in which to live and move and be comfortable with our being. Even a lovely 38' boat with three cabins is still a rather small place. Mary and I became close in a myriad of ways I cannot begin to describe. David still reminisces about our summer adventures and voyages.

We sold the Brandywine, Mary's boat a few months before she passed away. As of this writing she is moored at the Port of Poulsbo.

All good things come to an end. In the words of William Shakespeare, "The memory be green."

(15) DEATH WITH DIGNITY

Just as Mary and I ended our major fundraising efforts, which occupied most of the decade of the Eighties, another major opportunity appeared on the horizon.

In December of 1989, I was attending an informal luncheon for local Unitarian Universalist clergy when I received a telephone call.

I was pleased to hear the voice of my long time friend and colleague, the Rev. Dr. Ralph M. Mero, Jr. I had known Ralph since we were first year students together at Meadville Theological School in 1961. He graduated in 1965 and came to Kirkland, Washington to serve as minister at the Northlake Unitarian Universalist Church. He had subsequently pursued other professional interests, quite successfully and was now embarking on a new and what sounded like a very appealing project

He was creating an organization called Washington Citizens for Death with Dignity (WCDD), which he planned to register with the State of Washington as a Political Action Committee or PAC.

The plan was that WCDD would then file with the Secretary of State an Initiative to the Washington State Legislature titled the "Death With Dignity Act" – informally the DWD Act.

He wanted me to serve as Secretary of the organization.

I agreed, immediately and without hesitation. At the most basic level, I think I signed on so readily because I had faced the questions and conflicts of death albeit under different circumstances.

One simply cannot say "Yes" to Life without also being willing and able to say "Yes" to Death. The two constitute one seamless, inevitable, inescapable journey.

I also believe that the Second Principle of "justice, equity and compassion in human relations" mandates that a terminally ill person must be able to plan and carry out A Good Ending. No one can plan A Good Beginning. We can't order the circumstances of our birth. Yet we should have a determining voice as to the circumstances of our death, especially if we have a clearly terminal illness. The possibilities offered by modern medicine have blurred the line between life and death—raising the question of how long or under what circumstance do we prolong life?

Therefore we give little thought to the concept of A Good Death. There is simply no standard universal script as to what constitutes A Good Death. The choice is highly personal, but the choice needs to be available. During my years as a pastor I have witnessed a wide variation, ranging from an intentional, fatal dose of a prescription drug such as Seconal to a fierce battle to postpone death utilizing every possible medical technique, procedure and intervention.

The intent of the DWD Act was to make it possible for terminally ill, mentally competent persons who met certain strict requirements to avail themselves of physician-assisted aid in dying with dignity, by administering drugs that would lead to death.

Many proposed initiatives are filed with the Secretary of State but very few actually appear on the ballot at a general election and even fewer are approved by the voters. There are actually two formidable state-wide tasks: to secure the required number of signatures of registered voters, and then to staff and fund a persuasive state-wide campaign to prevail in a general election.

By the time I joined the campaign, the proposed law had been drafted and filed with the Secretary of State, as required by law. It was designated as Initiative 119.

To the extent that the media took notice, which was very slight indeed, it was immediately labeled "Assisted Suicide," and that label prevailed throughout the entire campaign

Leaving aside my wishes and desires, and concentrating on what was likely to happen, four tentative conclusions immediately came to mind, set forth here in no particular order.

- No far-reaching law even remotely similar to our proposed "Death with Dignity Act" had ever been offered to voters anywhere in the United States, and perhaps not anywhere in the world, and it was very unlikely to be enacted on the first try.

- Given that conclusion, the effort to promote such a law would in all probability let the Genie out of the bottle and change the prevailing culture permanently with regard to end-of-life decision-making and A Good Ending.

- I-119 presented a great opportunity to encourage every adult to have a Living Will and a Durable Power of Attorney for Health care, sometimes called a Health Care Proxy.

- Given the fact that I-120, concerning Abortion would likely be on the same ballot, opposition to both Initiatives would probably be harsh and mean-spirited. This was definitely not a campaign for the faint-hearted. I fully expected that as an ordained clergy person I would be especially vulnerable.

All four of these tentative conclusions proved to be accurate. Quite understandably they were not shared by the other key people in the campaign. I expected that, and was prepared, mentally and emotionally, to pursue a more modest vision, namely to "Let the Genie Out of the Bottle."

The leading organized opposition to I-119 emerged immediately, namely the Washington State Catholic Conference and an organization known as Human Life of Washington. Their first move was to file action in the Superior Court of Thurston County, challenging the State Attorney General's wording of the title of the initiative and the short summary. The challenge was dismissed by the court, out of hand, and 100,000 copies of the initiative were printed, each one bearing my name as Secretary of WCDD.

We rented a small office in downtown Seattle. The signature gathering, almost always the make-or-break feature of any initiative was successful and the proposed Death with Dignity Act went to the Legislature early in 1991. The Legislature took no direct action in the matter, and it was placed on the ballot for the general election to be held in November of 1991.

This meant a seismic shift from a signature-gathering effort to a state-wide political campaign, likely costing millions of dollars and a vast human effort.

We formed a small management team and I was one of several principal spokespersons. This meant giving persuasive speeches, participating in debates and writing articles. I appeared on radio and television, and in some cases these programs were broadcast throughout the world.

A principal activity was to organize Interfaith Clergy for "Yes" on I-119 which consisted of a state-wide group of several hundred clergy, mainly United Methodist, United Church of Christ and Unitarian Universalist. There were similar groups of other professions, including physicians and attorneys.

Separate from the formal campaign, I put together a packet of forms for the Living Will and the Durable Power of Attorney for Health Care (DPAHC) and conducted workshops far and wide. I urged people to actually complete the forms during the workshop and hundreds of people did that. The DPAHC at that time needed to be attested by a Notary Public so I obtained a Notary Public Commission from the State of Washington. Spreading this person-to-person awareness was one of the most satisfying aspects of the campaign, and I continued doing that long after the vote.

The campaign was very intense. We had the dual task of educating voters and seeking their support, while responding to the opposition. During the final days of the campaign, there was world-wide media interest. Television crews were interviewing each other while waiting to interview me. They were curious as to why there was such widespread interest.

Even though I-119 was defeated, 54% to 46%, the Genie was indeed let out of the bottle, never to be put back. Voters in Oregon subsequently approved a DWD Act which has been in effect for several years. Then, in 2008, voters in Washington State approved a far better DWD Act.

From my perspective this was one of the most significant and rewarding projects of my entire life. When someone is faced with a clearly terminal illness, the widest possible range of options and choices should be available to them and their loved ones. My parents, both of whom experienced terminal illnesses, should have had a wider range of options rather than the horrible death which came to both of them They might not have availed themselves of Death with Dignity, yet the option should have been available to them, and should be available to me if and when I am ever in such a situation.

Principal credit is due Dr. Mero, who envisioned the project and was the driving force throughout.

[16] THE BELLTOWN YEARS

People's Memorial Association (PMA), established in 1939 and headquartered in Seattle, is the largest memorial society in the United States, and on the continent it is second only to the one in Vancouver. PMA is not a political organization and did not formally endorse Initiative 119. However, they featured the proposed Death With Dignity Act at their annual meeting in 1991 and many PMA members supported the initiative with their time, energy and money.

I had been on the Board of the Memorial Society of British Columbia and about 1992 was elected to the board of PMA. This was an especially difficult time for PMA. For more than fifty years they had enjoyed an exclusive contract with a family-owned funeral home. The family sold the business to new owners, who simply did not seem to comprehend the magnitude of the situation. PMA generated more business for them in one month than most funeral homes experience in an entire year.

When regular folks sat around the breakfast table or the dining room table or in their neighborhood coffee shop discussing Initiative 119, final arrangements often entered the conversation. One of the possible dimensions of A Good Ending is the possibility of not spending thousands of dollars on a conventional embalming and earth burial. As a result, PMA was attracting new members at a faster rate than ever before.

Gradually we weathered the storm of the transition and established a good working relationship with the new owners of the funeral home. By modernizing our incoming telephone system and increasing our computer capability we were able to enroll many more members. We issued Membership Number 100,000 to Washington Governor Mike Lowry. We commissioned a short video suitable to be shown at presentations to a wide variety of organizations. We were growing quite rapidly.

Meanwhile, there were early yet ominous warning signs on the home front. In the mid-1980s Mary had two major surgeries for a benign invasive tumor in her head. The procedures affected her in various ways and I don't feel that she ever recovered completely. She seemed to experience a significant decline of energy and interest.

I was spending more time managing and running the household. By late 1992 it seemed to me that we needed to make a basic change in our living situation. We were in a large house, built on five levels, with 21 steps from the street to the main entrance. We looked at retirement homes but decided that at age 67 we were not ready for such a move. The ones we visited seemed more suitable for people in their 80s. We visited one where a dear friend of many years had a lovely apartment. She said, in a very heavy German accent, "Marvin! You're too young to come here." She was quite correct.

We had enjoyed our apartment in Boston so we decided we would investigate apartments in Seattle. At that time, downtown Seattle was not nearly as developed as it is now, 17 years later. First Avenue in the downtown area was an unkempt, unstable area with much prostitution and drug dealing and other undesirable activities.

So, in true Titanium Magnolia fashion she made a careful detailed list of her needs and requirements, including a heated indoor swimming pool. We looked at several complexes in north Seattle but it quickly became obvious that we were not likely to find what we wanted. That was when we decided to look downtown. There were very few modern apartment buildings in downtown Seattle in 1993, other than the Grosvenor House on Wall Street, which had been built many years earlier.

There was, however, a rental high-rise building, Centennial Tower, at 2515 Fourth Avenue. This is between Wall Street and Vine Street, a short distance south of Denny Way, and within easy walking distance of Nordstrom and the Bon Marche on the south and the Seattle Center on the north.

We looked first at Apartment 1401, a very nice unit with two bedrooms and two bathrooms on the northeast corner of the building. It was bright and featured a 215 degree view of everything from the light at Duwamish Head north and east to the Vance Hotel on Stewart Street. Both mountain ranges, Puget Sound, the Space Needle, Queen Anne Hill, Lake Union, everything. The building had an indoor heated pool, an outdoor whirlpool, an exercise room, a large residents' lounge, underground parking and many other amenities.

We knew instantly that we had found our future home. We stayed there exactly ten years.

I knew without even thinking that weaning Mary from her beloved house was going to be a major proposition. She loved it. She had the accumulation of three generations, had lived in the same house for 26 years, and now had a rather low energy level.

Wisely, very wisely, I just stood by while she set her own pace. At the end of May we began sleeping downtown. She put the house on the market in October and it closed in early January. One of the truly significant advantages of this approach is that we were under no pressure to sell the house quickly, or to sell it at all for that matter. We owned it outright and could have retained ownership indefinitely. The overlap was a very wise decision—the only one that would have worked under the circumstances.

Our move downtown was a very personal decision. Many friends asked us what it was like. High-rise living in downtown Seattle was a new lifestyle in those days. Most of the apartment buildings were older and were low-rise or mid-rise at best.

Our three years in downtown Boston had prepared us for this move. It is a very different way of life. For openers, it is never dark downtown, never quiet downtown and always dirty. Many people who took apartments at Centennial Tower simply could not cope with the normal sounds of the city: police cars, ambulances, fire engines, garbage trucks, delivery trucks, nighttime maintenance and repairs, late shift workers going and coming, revelers, the list goes on and on.

The main attraction, of course, is proximity to shopping, museums, galleries, theaters, sports venues and the cultural life of a major city. Travel by car takes on a different meaning,

Another advantage was that the building, with more than two hundred units, had a full-time maintenance staff. I have never been adept at household maintenance, and admittedly do not want any part of it, so it was good to be relieved of that responsibility.

The rent was less than the income generated by the sale of the house, and there were no real estate taxes, insurance, or maintenance costs. The offset to this, a major one, was the temptation to eat out quite frequently. The kitchen in our apartment, and even in the penthouse unit on the roof, left much to be desired. Mary was largely a vegetarian and I am an avid meat-eater. Our building housed a delicatessen, a French bakery and a lovely Asian restaurant. We spent a not-so-small fortune on food. The restaurant even delivered hot, delicious meals to our apartment. It was probably not more than two minutes from their kitchen to our door.

Downtown living is relatively isolating. That is the main reason I didn't move back to Belltown after Mary's death. When you arrange people vertically, they become less interactive. Also, many units in our building were leased but rarely occupied by absentee tenants who used them only when they happened to be in town, which was rarely. Good friends of ours had such a unit.

* * *

Near-tragedy was in the offing.

David, 38, was living alone in a small house he had purchased on Arrowhead Point in Kenmore. One night, in mid-December of 1995, quite late he tripped on his dog's water dish and fell into the bath tub. He didn't realize that he was bleeding internally, quite seriously.

By happenstance, a friend who is a registered nurse encountered him in a grocery store and recognized immediately that he was ill. She took him to the Emergency Room of the nearest hospital, which was the Evergreen Medical Center in the Totem Lake neighborhood of Kirkland.

He was admitted and immediately placed in Critical Care, which at that time was one patient and one nurse in an individual cubicle. He was very ill indeed. We were told that 23 of 25 standard indicators were bad and several were very bad indeed.

His friends set up a motor home in a far corner of the hospital parking lot and maintained a constant vigil around the clock. Mary and I were there all day every day. Even the cashiers in the cafeteria were holding him in their thoughts.

The first challenge was to stop the bleeding, and this was accomplished successfully. This left an ominous second problem, a huge hematoma, described as being the size of a football, in his back. It had to be removed, otherwise death was the only possible outcome.

He had a coronary arrest, which presented further complications. He was not a good candidate for surgery.

As fate would have it, the surgeon on the case, Dr. James Myhre, was present at the Dedication of Allen-Gates Hall at Lakeside School, where his daughter was a student and he knew about Kent's death. One morning early, after making rounds, he called us aside and told us about that. He indicated, quietly and thoughtfully, that he simply had no choice but to go in and try to remove the hematoma.

"My expectation is that he will die on the operating table, yet I must give it a try. This afternoon after the rush of the day is over, and assuming I can get the team I want, I'm going in there."

Mary and I waited nervously in the Surgery Waiting Room. Quite soon, too soon we thought, Dr. Myhre appeared.

"It's out! The next 24 hours will tell the story."

The next afternoon he announced, "Finally, at long last, I am ready to say I think he will make it."

Needless to say, Mary and I were overjoyed.

David did recover, although not fully and completely. We leased a one bedroom apartment in our building and furnished it so he and we could have privacy yet be close together.

He had to learn to walk again. He was totally dedicated to the physical therapy and we spent hours in the Residents' Lounge, just walking, walking, walking for hours on end. It was observed that he wasn't progressing adequately and he had to have a vertebrectomy, which is a major surgery.

While all this was happening he reconnected with Alexis Johanson, a single mother in her mid-thirties with a son, Michael. She was working full-time and providing a loving, caring home and family for the two of them. They spent lots of time together, quite enjoyably, and rather quickly pooled their households in Kirkland.

We had promised David that when he recovered adequately we would go to Desolation Sound aboard Brandywine. We did that in the summer of 1996, our last major cruise aboard Mary's boat.

Numerous people were vital to the successful outcome of this near-tragedy.

David had excellent medical care from the staff at the Evergreen Medical Center. Not only did he have three successful surgeries, two of which were highly problematic, but the nurses in Critical Care were vital to his survival and especially his recovery. They worked tirelessly to wean him from the ventilator.

Bill Houff and I had been exchanging our journals for about seven years and his understanding and support during this time was immensely helpful. This meant I had someone with whom I could commiserate, openly and deeply and candidly. We talked frequently, sometimes several times a day, depending on the situation. Having a confidant with whom you can truly express your deepest feelings and anxieties is an enormous advantage. He kept me sane and grounded in reality.

We understand each other to this day, as he deals with serious medical issues, both for himself and Patty.

David's friends were enormously helpful. They read sea stories to him when he was in an induced coma. When he was finally able to have solid food, they broiled a steak in the motor home. They retrieved his beloved Alfa Romeo and brought it to the main entrance so he could see that it was alive and well and hear its distinctive purr.

Although Dr. Bradley Harris, our family physician, did not have David as a patient, and was not in the loop at Evergreen, he conferred with the medical staff and assured us that everything that could be done was being done and expertly.

Finally, friends and colleagues rallied to our side in abundance and offered encouragement and assistance and consolation and most of all, their loving care and concern. I will never forget Christmas Dinner in the cafeteria at Evergreen.

* * *

Life moved along slowly and gently, when a difficulty with my vision needed attention.

My eye problems have affected me since childhood. As noted earlier I gave up my study of physics because I could not see adequately to do the lab work.

While I was at Randolph-Macon my ophthalmologist, unable to diagnose my condition to his satisfaction, sent me to the Wilmer Eye Institute at Johns Hopkins University, in Baltimore.

The staff there found that I had keratoconus. This is a deformity of the cornea of the eye. An attempt was made to fit me with contact lenses but that technology was not sufficiently advanced.

I somehow managed to live with the situation, although with increasing difficulty, until about 1964 when a technician in Victoria fitted me successfully with a pair of contact lenses. I have worn one or two such lenses ever since.

Contact lens technology continued to advance and I was fitted and refitted continuously for thirty years.

However, by the spring of 1997 we had run out of options. I was faced with the probability of being unable to renew my driver's license.

I wrote a minister's column, From the Bosun's Chair, in the newsletter of University Unitarian Church, a description of what happened next.

"I had a corneal transplant on July 31. This procedure involves removing the cornea (the outer layer) of the eye and replacing it with the cornea of an eye donated by someone who has died.

"I waited the relatively short period of five weeks for an available eye from the eye bank. Yet even five weeks gave me a much deeper understanding of organ and tissue donation.

"What if my situation had been life-threatening? What if I had needed a heart or a kidney? What if no organ had been available? Every day I thought about how wonderful it would be to receive, from someone I didn't even know, the gift of renewed vision, possibly better vision than I have ever had.

"I am aware that many people have organ donor cards. But that fact alone is not enough! Talk with your family members and your health care proxy about your wishes and instructions. Make sure they know what you want and that they inform the appropriate medical personnel. In such situations, time is of the essence."

I recovered quite nicely and now have better vision than I have ever had in my entire life.

Yet this story contains one more important caution.

When I arrived at the hospital and was checking in for the transplant, they affixed a name band to my wrist. They did not ask me to verify the name and date of birth and I foolishly didn't look at the band.

I was in the prep room being readied when a staff person came and asked me my name and social security number. I gave it to them. A few minutes later a second staff person came and asked me the same thing. Again, I provided the information.

Then, Big Nurse appeared on the scene. She stood at the foot of the bed, arms folded across her ample chest and declared, in a loud voice: DOESN'T LOOK LIKE A 'MARY' TO ME!

They had misidentified me as Mary Hood Evans! They gave me another arm band, but with her date of birth! They never did get it correct!

So, if you are conscious and have your wits about you, ALWAYS verify the name and patient number and date of birth.

In the early summer of 1997, the Rev. Dr. Peter Raible, senior minister at University Unitarian Church since February 1, 1961, announced his resignation. Ministerial transition in a large congregation after a long and successful ministry is precarious at best. Bill Houff was 68 and had retired to Spokane yet he had done four successful stints as an Accredited Interim Minister and was still quite alert and energetic. I thought he would be an excellent choice yet I had to move very carefully and cautiously. As a Minister Associate and voting member of the congregation, I was under the mandate of the Unitarian Universalist Ministers Association to stay aloof from the inner workings of the church. I knew from back channel sources that he was being considered but I kept my own counsel.

Finally, the phone rang. "Marvin, this is Bill." I knew instinctively why he was calling and what he had on his mind.

"Hi. I've been waiting for this call."

Obviously taken aback, he exclaimed, "You have?"

"Yes. Carry on."

He explained that he had been approached to be the AIM at UUC. No surprise there.

"That's interesting. I have two questions for you."

"Go ahead."

"First question. Is Kaky [his wife's daughter, the Rev. Kathleen Mc-Tigue, UU minister in New Haven, CT) interested in the job?'

"No, she wants to stay in New Haven until her girls finish high school."

"Good. Second question. If the job is offered to you, are you prepared to accept.?"

"Yes."

"Good. Proceed."

"Thanks."

"Call me if you have any questions. Good-bye"

"Good-bye."

Bill took up his duties in September and we had a most interesting time together. Large congregations that have had the same minister for fifteen years or more develop numerous "inscrutable mysteries." Institutional memory is in short supply and the landscape is alive with land mines and UXBs - Unexploded Bombs. An AIM needs all the help he or she can get. I had learned that lesson in Devon, PA twenty years earlier. Bill and I conferred frequently, sometimes four or five times a day. Mary was enormously helpful because her knowledge of the situation was phenomenal. We were together almost fifty years before her mind failed and I never knew her to forget anyone's name and something about them. Never. People who hadn't been around for decades suddenly reappeared. Mary knew them and had an uncanny sense of what their agendas might be. She was correct every time.

Bill had a one year agreement with an option for a second year. The first year was quite difficult, as is frequently the case. Dr. Raible had been there more than thirty-five years. The second year went much better and an excellent Ministerial Search Committee, chaired by Dr. Bruce Davis, selected an excellent candidate.

The Rev. Jon M. Luopa, then serving a congregation in Hartford, CT, was on my list of persons worthy of consideration and he was called in the spring of 1999.

* * *

Then Mary had a mini-stroke, called a Transient Ischemic Attack or TIA, a spontaneous hip fracture, and was diagnosed with Parkinson's disease and early dementia.

(17) A GREAT ADVENTURE COMES TO AN END

Mary's health continued to decline. She never regained the ability to walk after the hip replacement and we reluctantly had to put her in a wheel chair. This was a very difficult decision for David and me, yet I simply could not handle the situation any other way. She could not propel herself so I bought a small, light weight transfer chair, which is what she used from then on. It was easily maneuvered in the apartment and easy to put in and out of the car. Taking her for doctor's appointments and to the hair salon became increasingly difficult.

We bought an electric recliner and she spent most of the day in our living room. About 2001 we moved to a handicapped accessible apartment on the sixth floor, losing our view but gaining wider doors and a roll-in shower.

Her situation was completely confining for her and increasingly confining for me. I could occasionally walk up to Nordstrom and have a cup of coffee, or even go to a concert at Benaroya Hall yet my world was quite limited. I made arrangements with a commercial home care company for someone to come for four hours on Sunday, so I could go to church.

I came to realize, all too slowly, that the situation was getting out of control. Mary was understandably quite restless at night, so that I could not sleep adequately. I bought a single bed, put it in the second bedroom, and installed a wireless intercom. That was what Peter Raible called a noble idea and, like most such ideas, it didn't work.

Finally, belatedly, I realized I needed what virtually everyone needs in a similar situation. I needed a competent, professional assessment from a care management specialist who had no emotional involvement in the situation and could, therefore, look at it professionally and objectively.

I arranged for such an assessment and it was one of the wisest expenditures of my entire life. It was absolutely priceless.

The highly experienced care manager, Judy Kimmerer, of Adult Care Resources, came and interviewed us and asked all the pertinent questions in a very sensitive, caring thoroughly competent, professional manner.

Her recommendation was that we needed Assisted Living and that, ideally, we should try to move to such a facility together. It seemed obvious to her that no other arrangement would work for me, given our devotion to each other.

Three years earlier David had purchased a home in Eagledale, on Bainbridge Island. It made sense to move closer to him. He knew about a small, relatively new facility in Winslow, the Wyatt House Retirement Center. I went and looked at it and also the Madison Avenue Retirement Center, owned by the same company.

The Wyatt House had very few units designed for two people so we decided to shoehorn ourselves into a one bedroom corner unit with a total of 300 square feet. We had a living room with a hot plate, microwave and refrigerator, and a large bathroom with a roll-in shower. The bedroom was just large enough for a queen size bed and adequate space to maneuver the small transport wheel chair. Very compact yet adequate.

We moved to the Wyatt House on February 4, 2003. The staff immediately put both of us under the care of Sundance Rogers, MD, at the Virginia Mason Clinic Winslow. This was an amazingly fortuitous development.

I continued to be Mary's primary caregiver yet we had several significant advantages including three meals a day in the very nice dining room and staff available at all times if needed.

Most fortunately I had the skills to be her caregiver, and I was both happy and proud about that. The September 2004 issue of O, The Oprah Magazine, had an article contending that "Men Are from Mars, Period," and must be changed to think and act more like they were from Venus.

To the magazine's credit, they printed my rebuttal.

> "[Your article] struck me as simplistic. My wife and I have been married for 51 years, and it has been a fabulous adventure. During that time, she has taught me a lot about Venus and I have taught her much about Mars. She now has a fatal illness, and I am her primary caregiver. That daunting task requires both Mars and Venus - I would not have it to be otherwise.

Rev Marvin D. Evans
Bainbridge Island, Washington

When Mary was diagnosed with Parkinson's Disease and early dementia, she made a very careful study of the various medications usually prescribed for such diseases. She took Aricept for a while but discontinued it because of the consequences, mistakenly and misleadingly called side-effects. She never took any of the medications prescribed for Parkinson's Disease. This was a very unusual approach yet typical of her careful, measured response to her diagnoses. Every medication she studied had serious consequences and as was so frequently the case with many aspects of her life, she decided to take her own road.

She was totally aware as to the road she was taking, namely her own specific pathway to what she envisioned as A Good Ending.

She functioned relatively well through the spring and summer. On August 8, 2003, we celebrated our Fiftieth Wedding Anniversary with a lovely party in the dining room of the Wyatt House.

During the winter months, her condition deteriorated steadily. I was there with her and needed to preserve my sanity so I bought a computer and Internet access. I had never seen a web page and I spent countless hours on the Internet, a kid with a new toy. It was a lifesaver.

By late winter her mind was basically gone yet she was quite lucid about not wanting to linger fruitlessly. She especially wanted

David and Alexis and me, as she put it hundreds of times, "to get on with our lives."

Years earlier, at the time of the Death with Dignity campaign in 1990-1991, she read Final Exit, and many articles about end-of-life decision making. She decided, firmly and resolutely, that when her time came she would stop eating.

She talked about that through the spring and summer but David was horrified by the prospect so I just told her the time wasn't right.

One of the tragedies for me was that she kept saying, over and over, "You're a woman, aren't you?"

I would then explain to her carefully and thoughtfully that I was Marvin, her husband of fifty years.

A few minutes later she would say, "You're a woman, aren't you?"

After many instances of this I finally gave up and said, "Yes, my name is Katharine. I'm your caregiver."

She never asked the question again. She died with me as Katharine, her caregiver.

This was an incredibly trying experience for me, yet one aspect of dealing with a loved one whose mind has faded. Perhaps the Venus in me was stronger than the Mars in that particular situation. We loved each other dearly.

Early in September, Dr. Rogers referred her case to Hospice of Kitsap County. Two staff members came and interviewed both of us, separately and together, and admitted her to care.

The following evening, Saturday, September 11, 2004, she said quietly, after a very light dinner, that she had eaten her last meal.

We cleared space in the living room for a standard hospital bed and she passed away in that bed at 5:35 p.m. on Thursday, September 30, 2004.

My journal entry for Monday, September 27, reads, in part:

> "I note again that this is what I call A NATURAL DEATH. Perhaps there is an even better description. I'll need to think about that.

"Even in theistic terms, Mary had been a good and faithful Servant and I'm sure God would have no problem welcoming her home perhaps a bit earl—whenever her earthly journey was truly completed and well-done.

"After all, if you assume a Creator, that Creator gave us a mind/brain and expects us to look, listen, think, reflect and act. That's what Mary did!"

The most appropriate thing I can say is that she did it her way. She lived by her principles and standards and beliefs more completely and unfailingly than anyone I have ever known. She walked the walk. She was a living embodiment of the Seven Unitarian Universalist Principles.

She left me with definite verbal ideas as to what she wanted to have happen after her death.

She had three major instructions:

She wanted a Memorial Service at University Unitarian Church, on Sunday afternoon, with essentially the regular Order of Worship but instead of a sermon she wanted two brief "Perspectives" by the senior minister, the Rev. Jon M. Luopa and our dear friend, the Rev. Dr. William H. Houff. I invited the Rev. Alicia M. Grace to participate. The service was held on Sunday, October 31, 2004, and was an excellent celebration of her life.

She wanted me to make every reasonable effort to carry out the financial arrangements she and I had agreed on even before we were married. They were incredibly complicated but the goal was attained after nine months of careful, friendly litigation in the Chancery Division of the Circuit Court of Henrico County, Virginia, where her father's will had been admitted to probate in 1936.

And as she put it scores of times, she hoped David and Alexis and I would "get on with our lives."

As it turned out, both Mr. Luopa and Dr. Houff told her all-time favorite story about herself.

From her earliest days in the elementary grades at Ginter Park School, she had been a self-designated defender and protector of the Queen's English. Her spoken words and her writing were impeccable.

Late one night she and I were in the study at the house. The telephone rang and she answered.

It was a VERY obscene phone call. The four letter words and the phone sex continued far longer than I would have tolerated.

At last, in her finest, most genteel Virginia accent she asked, "With whom did you wish to speak?"

The caller, obviously thrown off balance, exclaimed, "Lady, you must be crazy!" and hung up.

Like her final passage, it was vintage Mary Hood Evans.

(18) SAYING "YES"

Five years later, Mary's hopes have been realized. David has found a fulfilling life managing his varied financial interests while teaching young people the art and skill of sailing, occasionally assisting with yacht deliveries and supporting Alexis Johanson in her new ventures. At this writing she is an outstanding student at Arizona State University. This was one of Mary's foremost hopes and desires. David is also supporting Alexis' son Michael Johanson, a senior at ASU.

After Mary's death, I did not need to be in an assisted living facility so I decided to stay on Bainbridge Island and on December 1, 2004 moved to a very nice apartment in a nearby complex called Island Homestead. I thought seriously about returning to Belltown, yet it is not the most appropriate location for an unmarried person of my age.

I was finally free to become much more active at Cedars Unitarian Universalist Church. This is a vibrant, active, thriving congregation where I have many interesting, caring friends.

Through the magic of the Internet I met a family who lives in Halifax, Nova Scotia. As a result I have fallen in love with the Atlantic provinces of Canada, especially Nova Scotia and Prince Edward Island (P.E.I.). Through their hospitality and generosity, we have traveled very extensively in the four provinces, the two just mentioned plus New Brunswick and Newfoundland.

I feel at home with the people and landscape of the seaport town of Lunenburg, NS. One might think I was born nearby. We have been to P.E.I. three times and I have read twelve of the 20th century novels of Lucy Maud Montgomery. These include the eight Anne Shirley ("Anne of Green Gables") novels, the three Emily Byrd Starr novels, and L.M.'s favorite, "Story Girl."

Giving myself permission to read fiction is a very special treat. For sixty years I had felt compelled to read history, biography and memoirs, psychology and current affairs. Now I can see how fiction also informs us of real life joys and conflicts, yet in different ways than non-fiction. Both forms stretch my thinking and enrich my life. I wish I had started reading fiction much earlier.

I still have my quiet time most mornings, and have recently added a second introductory reading, along with "Look to This Day!"

It is a hymn entitled "Just as Long as I Have Breath," by Alicia S. Carpenter:

> Just as long as I have breath,
> I must answer, "Yes," to life;
> though with pain I made my way,
> still with hope I meet each day.
> If they ask what I did well,
> Tell them I said, "Yes," to life.
> Just as long as vision lasts,
> I must answer, "Yes," to truth;
> in my dream and in my dark,
> always that elusive spark.
> If they ask what I did well,
> tell them I said, "Yes," to truth.
> Just as long as my heart beats,
> I must answer, "yes," to love;
> disappointment pierced me through,
> still I kept on loving you.
> If they ask what I did well,
> tell them I said, "Yes," to love.

[19] REFLECTIONS ON AN UNCOMMON LIFE

As I work my way through my 85th year, I am more inclined than ever to "Look to This Day," with very keen emphasis on the word THIS. Long range plans seem less relevant than ever.

I am, however, filled with joy and appreciation and even awe for the rich, full, satisfying life that has been mine, and still is mine.

The ancient Funk & Wagnalls Standard Dictionary (1966) that my dear friend, Alan Miller, picked up at a sale and passed along to me defines the word "unique" as follows:

> Unique: Being the only one of its kind; being without equal; singular; uncommon; rare.

Based on the limited scope of my own experience, coupled with a lifetime addiction to newspapers, my life strikes me as having been uncommon, rare, infrequent or unusual. Singular in the sense that I have never met anyone who had a reasonably similar experience.

"Letting Go of Yesterday" truly defines and describes my life. It is the principal, compelling reason why this memoir is entitled "Pearl's Boy." She instilled that view of life in my selfhood before I reached adolescence, and it serves me well. This concept of "Letting Go" is developed by The Dalai Lama and Howard C. Cutler in their book, "The Art of Happiness," which has had, and continues to have, a huge impact in my life. It stands out among the books I have read during sixty-five years dedicated to "Salvation by Bibliography" or "You Are What You Read."

Being able to retire at age forty-one is relatively uncommon. The most significant factor here is that Mary and I retired with a definite, well-defined goal in mind. We wanted to work in the volunteer sector, full-time and purposefully, devoting our abilities and energy to things we deemed important.

As written here, there were many such activities. For myself, the most important one, by far, was Washington State Initiative 119, the proposed Death with Dignity Act of 1990 - 1991. This is the public effort for which I would most like to be remembered.

Looked at statistically, being an active, devoted member of a Unitarian Universalist congregation is very uncommon. The U.S. Population Clock shows approximately three hundred million inhabitants. There are about 220,000 of us, far less than one-tenth of one percent. Statistically insignificant.

My fifty-one years as an active member of Unitarian Universalist congregations describes and defines who I am as a person. The effort is not entirely successful yet the central goal of my life is to live according to the Seven Principles. Mary was more skilled at the task yet we walked the walk together, encouraging each other, nurturing each other, caring for each other, loving each other. She walked the walk more effectively than anyone else I have ever known. Now that she is gone, I continue the journey with my companions in Cedars Unitarian Universalist Church, which draws its membership primarily from the City of Bainbridge Island and North Kitsap County, across Puget Sound from Seattle.

There is one additional uncommon factor that is highly personal yet also highly relevant to the story of Pearl's Boy.

I have never in my entire life had a financial problem of any kind. Long before I met and married Mary I made out quite well with whatever money I had. I lived in rooming houses and ate in boarding houses and shared very rudimentary apartments with friends.

Mary and I were not wealthy. We simply lived within our means. We never had a debt we couldn't pay. We never once in fifty years had an argument or even a serious disagreement about money. We simply didn't spend money we didn't have.

I consider myself to have been uncommonly fortunate in this regard. I have a strong, pervasive feeling that it has spared me from a wide variety of strains and stresses. It has been a very important aspect of my uncommon life.

Being a Unitarian Universalist clergy person is uncommon and has been my professional identity for almost half a century.

Keeping a daily journal and exchanging that journal weekly with Bill Houff, my colleague, confidant and friend has been and continues to be a very rich and uncommon experience.

Lastly, saying, "Yes" to life also means saying, "Yes" to death. The two are inseparable parts of a single journey. I hope I will be able to say, "Yes" to death and have A Good Ending.

So be it!

KENT HOOD EVANS MEMORIAL

KENT HOOD EVANS, the son of Marvin Davis and Mary Hood Evans, was born March 18, 1955, in Richmond Virginia. His death on May 28, 1972 was the result of a mountain-climbing accident on Mt. Shuksan in the Cascade Mountains of Washington State. In addition to his parents, Kent is survived by his younger brother, David.

Kent's family has lived in Seattle, Washington since 1967. Prior to that time Kent's father was minister of the Unitarian Church of Victoria in Victoria, British Columbia, from 1963 to 1967. Kent attended Monterey and Glenlyon Schools in Victoria.

At the time of his death Kent was a junior at the Lakeside School in Seattle. In the fall of 1972 it was announced that he was one of Lakeside's eleven semifinalists in the National Merit Scholarship tests.

In addition to his school activities, Kent was an enthusiastic, tireless worker in several political campaigns and numerous computer projects. He became an avid backpacker and joined the Mountaineers so that he could choose from a weekly smorgasbord of trips. He enrolled in a basic mountain-climbing course at the University of Washington and was on the final class climb at the time of his death.

KENT HOOD EVANS
(March 18, 1955 - May 28, 1972)
MEMORIAL SERVICE HELD IN
THE THEODORE AIKEN McKAY CHAPEL
LAKESIDE SCHOOL

Seattle, Washington
Monday, June 5, 1972

PARTICIPANTS:

The Reverend Robert L. Fulghum
Minister, Edmonds, Unitarian Church and
Director of Visual Arts, Lakeside School

Sally Ambrose
Lakeside School, Class of 1972, Flutist

A. D. Ayrault, Jr., Headmaster, Lakeside School

INVOCATION: Reverend Fulghum

We have come together – on this elegant evening on the edge of high summer – to honor the memory of Kent Evans.

And though it is his death that brings us here, it is not his death that deserves our attention.

Not at all!

Rather we have come to celebrate his life – as best we can. To remember him as a student, as a colleague, as a peer. To remember him as a friend, as a brother and of course, as a son.

We have come to share memories and anecdotes, to express feelings – and admiration, above all.

Everybody who knew Kent knew that he was more than sensitive to the painful side of being alive – and so tears are certainly appropriate here.

And everybody who knew Kent knew that he fully appreciated the silly side of the human race – and so laughter is also ok.

Likewise it is also ok to speak intelligently and seriously for above all, Kent Evans appreciated the rigorous intellect and the disciplined mind.

I say these things – they will sound familiar to some of you – for Kent had appreciated the way in which the Lakeside School community had honored the memory of Bruce Burgess, a teacher much beloved by us all, who died earlier this year.

And we would do no less to honor Kent in the spirit that he appreciated, with respect for the whole person, with respect for a young man experiencing the full flower of his manhood.

And this will not be an easy task, not because there is so little to say, but because there is so very, very, very much to say about Kent Evans.

It is so easy to forget that he was just 2 months away from 17, for his life was so very full – his biography reads like that of a man twice his age. It would be the envy of most of us.

His dying so young is difficult to understand – to grasp – to accept.

Death is always an enigma.

The human race has been struggling with, wrestling with, that enigma for a long, long time and will struggle with it for a long time yet to come.

When it comes to dealing with the meaning of death and the why of death, the wisest words are still those written about 3,000 years ago contained in the Book of Ecclesiastes:

> "I turned and saw under the Sun, that the race is not to the swift, nor the battle to the strong, neither yet bread to the wise, nor riches to men of understanding, nor yet favor to mean of skills; but time and chance happeneth to them all.
>
> For everything there is a season, and a time for all things under heaven.
>
> A time to be born, and a time to die."

And a more contemporary writer echoed those words with these:

"With no say in the matter we are brought to life. Nobody asked us. And with no vote nor rebuttal, nor reservations, we come to die."

And it seems to me we have no choice but to finally accept the ways of an ongoing universe, which is, no doubt, in its mysterious way, working itself out as it should.

MEDITATION: Sally Ambrose, Flutist

PERSPECTIVE: Mr. Ayrault

To those of us at Lakeside, Kent Evans was ubiquitous. Not that his Middle School math students or his friends might use that word exactly, but how else, for example, could you explain Kent's constant company at Middle School lunch when he was presumably involved in a demanding academic program of his own at the Upper School? Some might call it a masterful blend of maneuvering, manipulation, and political skill, but I choose to think of it as all of that ... plus ubiquity.

Kent was able to well ... arrange things, and as a result, an ultimate practitioner of the art, he managed to work it out so that the interests of other people, the school and Kent Evans were served with mutual benefit. But somehow the excellence of his performance and the totality of his involvement make our reflections merge into an impression of simultaneous presence and achievement.

It fits nicely to imagine him having discovered some remarkable secret that enabled him to do several things at once indeed, even in different locations. I picture him chuckling quietly at the rest of us while making that remarkable and striking head of his materialize like Alice in Wonderland's grinning Cheshire Cat, only to dissolve into another time, place and adventure. What is the basis for such conjecture? Let me give you some sense of the evidence.

From one of his teachers:

The really remarkable thing is how he managed everything. He was taking Advanced Placement Chemistry, a college course, with a great deal of lab work, and Honors Math. These two alone keep most talented students very busy. He did lots of computer work, including contracts with outside agencies, taught math and computer classes at the Upper and Middle Schools, did a major share of the year's scheduling, and was out every weekend hiking or climbing - and he did all these things unusually well. He always had time to stop and talk every morning, and, incredibly, never seemed busy or harassed or impatient. He always, invariably, was cheerful and smiling.

From Another:

One of the best computer crises was the DECTAPE incident. Paul Allen, Rick Weiland, Bill Gates and Kent had long been working together to get, at a very low price, the entire DEC-TAPE supply of bankrupt Computer Center Corporation. Finally Bill and Kent made a breakthrough and bought them without the knowledge of Paul and Rick.

For some reason Kent's plan, involved hiding the DECTAPES in the back of one of the school's teletypes. The plan backfired when Paul and Rick found the tapes and hid them somewhere else. Kent was livid and threatened to go to court and to the police to get them back. After several days of wait and many hours of arbitration and negotiation, a truce was reached. Thanks to Kent's follow-through and carefully planned business letters, Kent and Bill went on to sell the tapes at a considerable profit.

When Kent was working on the Middle School schedule, some of his young friends there, Brad Augustine, Drake Smith and Chris Larson, promised him a pair of hiking boots if he could cajole the computer into writing special schedules for them. The task turned out to be impossible, so Kent programmed the computer to print on their schedules: "SORRY. I DIDN'T HAVE TIME – THE SCHEDULING PHANTOM. " Unfortunately, by that time we were all pretty tired, and his program went a bit awry, printing several of his messages on the wrong schedules.

The result was a few rather confused students, asking who this "Scheduling Phantom" was, and what it was he didn't have time to do.

From a poem about Kent by one of his friends with whom he worked on that schedule:

So clear to me still is your voice announcing in distress that the only kid who had no English class was named, alas, Lisa Ayrault.

Another said:

He had a great sense of being self-reliant, or self-dependent, or of feeling that one took care of things himself and didn't expect help from others. As an example, on the St. Helen's trip of last December, we tried to wait out a storm by camping down in the trees, on the snow. In the middle of the night in the wind, tents were tearing because of gusts and it was pouring rain.

Most of us had our tents literally filling up with water. Kent's tent tore, so he couldn't use it. He came over to my tent and said that people were having trouble with their tents, should we do anything? He carefully never said anything about his own tent. I had him go around and check the state of tents so he wouldn't be standing around in the rain, and only when he came back and reported a wet situation did I quiz him on his tent specifically and find out it was in bad shape. When we were hiking out that night because of the rain, he had snowshoe binding problems and couldn't keep one on. He didn't curse or complain or ask for help, but simply kept struggling in wet snow more than knee deep in the pitch dark. By the next day he was ready to go again.

From an Upper School teacher:

I would run into him down at the Middle School, always working with kids in the computer room. He'd always be looking for a ride back to the Upper School, but after lunch, thank you, theirs being better, he thought.

Here is what one of those Middle School students had to say:

The first day I met Kent, I admired him. The way he stuck up for what he thought was right, and the way he taught me to use the computer, both made me happy. When there was a job to do, like teaching kids at the Middle School how to use the computer, or telling me what was wrong with my program, Kent was always there with a helping hand. Kent gave me my first computer job, working and reading traffic tapes. I was quite honored when he asked me, little me, to do a computer job for him, and when he told me I would get paid, I was even happier. Kent could explain things better than anyone else.

From another of his teachers:

I have a general impression of a strongly emerging individual. He was seriously interested in teaching, spending much time and effort on his Middle School teaching assignments. He integrated his reading and his experience in this area. What was really impressive was his ability (which few of us ever have) to be amused by his initial failures; as, for example, when all the students in his Middle School computer class failed the test he had given them. He and Tim Thompson used to compete over who was the least effective teacher. As a result, through the term he was able to recognize and appreciate his own progress in organizing and structuring his teaching for the individual student's benefit.

He even organized a "son of" Teaching Theory class for the spring term so that he could further pursue these goals. He was also instrumental in organizing a new course for next year – a sort of Student Review Board to work on educational problems particular to Lakeside. He acted as a conscience for the school, the students, Dan Ayrault, and the Review Board."

From another:

"Kent probably tied up more time on school phone lines than all other students combined. When we first started looking into the possibility of buying a computer, there was a flood of long distance calls from as far away as Georgia, asking for Mr. Kent Evans of the Lakeside School. At the time Kent was a

9th grader, but that didn't strike him as being of any particular significance. He was a great schemer and entrepreneur, one of the prime movers in the Lakeside Programming Group. He became fascinated by the legal aspects of their subsequent battle with Information Sciences, Inc., over their payroll project and dreamed up all kinds of ways to get even with the company – most of which he later thought better of."

He was pragmatic and could adjust his plans and dreams to fit reality. Witness this story:

This spring I tried to get him to come on the 9th and 10th grade beach hikes as a cooking group leader since he had gotten so good at it. He felt committed to the climbing course, however, which went out every weekend. He did go with me to buy the food, and enjoyed the rushing around getting such enormous quantities of food. We got so we were trying to set speed records on leaving the school, buying the food and getting back. On the last trip we did the door-to-door operation in 27 minutes for $128.00 worth of food for the 10th grade beach hike. We had gotten to be such good customers at Albertson's that they gave us two gallons of ice cream free the last time. He figured we could eat it. After seven dishes of ice cream he started to realize how much ice cream two gallons amount to.

And so it went, the Lakeside life and schedule of this remarkable person. And throughout, graced by unusual maturity, balance and sensitivity for the feeling of others. He could drive a hard financial bargain at one moment, and appear quietly the next expressing concern that all was well.

As we grope for perspective this evening, let one thing be clear, this was a rich, full life - and what a gift for all of us to be a part of it.

AFFIRMATION: Reverend Fulghum

The first time I ever had any personal contact with Kent was several years ago when I went to an organizing meeting of the Washington Democratic Council at the Seattle Center.

And there, seated among piles of politicians and party workers and representatives of the press and all sorts of hangers-on, was this funny looking little kid armed with a pencil and a notebook and a grin and a gleam in his eye as though he knew what was going on.

I sat down beside him and soon found much to my amazement that he did know what was going on – that he knew more about what was going on than I did. He knew who was who and what the power struggles were likely to be and what the platform would become. His prediction of what their platform would have to be – pragmatically was right on target.

That was Kent Evans – thirteen years old.

I think he knew more about politics that I will ever know.

The next contact I had with him was when he came to the art studio to take graphics. He immediately declared for my benefit that he was the worst artist in Lakeside School, but that he would do the course and I would have to put up with it.

As always, Kent spoke the truth – he was the worst artist in Lakeside School. And he did do the course. And what he turned out we carefully hid – it was so awful to look at.

But the thing that intrigued me was his interest in the technical processes – the nature of ink and the nature of sharpening tools.

But beyond that the thing that most intrigued me was how acutely he observed me as a teacher and how interested he was in the way I went about teaching art and why. And he contributed much to my tradition of having my courses evaluated when he said he thought it would be a good idea to ask the students what they thought about what I was doing.

The last personal contact I had with Kent was after a faculty meeting when he and his colleagues had presented a plan for teacher evaluation at Lakeside. Now you have to understand that at the same time he was working on a plan for teacher evaluation, he was also negotiating full tilt with the administration to do all the scheduling for the whole school for the next year and to be paid for it. As I understand it, the Friday before he left he had driven home a contract which I think the school may still be a little uneasy about. When I asked him corning out of the faculty meeting what his reaction was to how the faculty accepted the proposal, he said in a very kind and benevolent but slightly humorous way, "Well, they've got a lot to learn."

And as usual he spoke the truth.

Stories about Kent Evans like this and the ones Dan shared with you could to on and on and on. They are very typical. So often when you do a memorial service you have to reach for the edge of truth to find something to say. In Kent's case, the truth is that this is an incredible young man. Only after we have stopped and taken a hard look at all the places he was and all the things he did and all the people's lives he touched, do we realize how very special he was.

I've talked with friends at length this week, and time and time again, the same qualities come through – an abiding interest in everything he touched – a concern for excellence – a demand for excellence – not only for himself, but for his teachers, his peers, his colleagues. And all the while this almost fey sense of warmth and good humor that somehow served as a shield against being a misanthrope and against cynicism.

It is a good thing that Kent had sound judgment and that he was basically honest, for as one of his friends said about him. He had all the makings of a great criminal genius. He was always figuring out ways to break complex computer codes and how to fuzz up Fortran computer logic and how to get back at corporations he thought were dishonest or unethical – and he could have done it and they would have been sorry too.

He proved himself – before he was 17 – an able businessman, able to handle books and contracts and detailed negotiations. He proved himself – before he was 17 – a searcher of law books, a teacher, an outdoorsman of merit, a friend.

One look in his room at home – a small room, absolutely jammed with books on every imaginable subject, stacked with computer cards and computer print-outs and littered with camping gear and bits and parts of mysterious machinery, and you know that you are in the presence of a young man pushing his resources and his capacities as far and as hard and as fast as he possibly could. In fact, the only complaint, the only negative thing, that I could get out of any of his friends or his family, was that they simply could not keep up with his pace.

Not only was he deeply involved in the present, but he was busy laying plans for the future; he was going to Peru, and he was going to buy a Land Rover, and he had hikes and climbs to the Cascades planned, and he had all sorts of wild money–making schemes, and he was going to take an adventure into politics, and one thing his family and friends found out, was that these dreams had an amazing way of coming true and were never to be taken lightly. He made them happen.

One theme runs through everything I have said about Kent and everything that Dan said about Kent, and that is his exhilaration in the face of challenge. He was, for example, an expert sailor. Not one of your lazy-days, calm-water, fool-around sailors, but his family can well testify, he couldn't come near another boat without seeing if he could get in a race. His father tells with great pride of a time when a storm came upon them and Kent took the helm with great exhilaration and not only took them safely through the storm but did something his father would never dare to do and that's sail right up to the dock so you could step off if you wanted to.

Kent's friends confirm this characteristic by saying that he was never so happy as when a situation got frantic or confused or complicated, be it a math problem, or Lakeside scheduling, or a business deal, or logistics for a computer program. He liked it fast and heavy, and in turmoil.

And it is finally to that particular point, that response to challenge, that I want to address my final remarks. Not that by any means I have exhausted or we have exhausted what there is to say. Only that there is a time to bring words to an end, knowing that, especially in Kent's case, no matter what we say, it is not enough.

When I first read the account of Kent's death in the newspaper, my response was to wonder what he was doing up there in the mountains – Mt. Shuksan is not a Sunday hike! It is a serious climb. It requires, skill, knowledge of mountaineering, faith in your own resources – a lot of stamina.

Kent was not particularly athletic. He was not particularly well–coordinated. To look at him you would not immediately think, "there's a mountaineer."

What was he doing up there? And he was climbing with university students – with people who were older than he – whose physical skills were more mature than his.

Why was he there? That's always the question that is asked of a mountaineer, why do men climb mountains anyhow? Well, the truth of the matter is, most men don't. A lot of men who start out to climb mountains don't last very long and then there are those who choose not to climb mountains, but to be mountaineers, which is something else. To carefully, deliberately, thoughtfully and with great purpose, go to the mountains as a way of being alive, finding something there that they can't find anywhere else.

I guess it is because mountaineering offers what is perhaps the purest form of human challenge. There's no fame or fortune. Not even conquest often. All the challenge that's offered is the challenge of testing one's resources to the limit. The challenge of finally conquering oneself.

The mountaineer is called upon to be an athlete to be sure, but he is also called upon to be explorer and cartographer and pioneer. He is called upon to be a geologist and a doctor and a rescuer, a meteorologist. He is called upon to be a botanist, a photographer, a philosopher, a cook, and most often a friend. And frequently he is called upon to fill all these roles in a matter of hours.

There are a lot of romantic cliches about mountaineering. In Kent Evan's case, they hold true. James Ramsay Uhlman sums up mountaineering in his classic the Age of Mountaineering in this way:

The making of a mountaineer depends not so much on what a man does, but on what he is; not on what vertical cliffs or dizzy summits he has conquered, but on what he carries with him in his mind and heart. No matter what the experience of the mountaineer, all have found the struggle for the summit worth doing, for its own sake, and in the end, it has always been the spirit of the mountaineers rather than their achievements, that has given meaning and stature to their enterprises. It is the ultimate wisdom of the mountains that man is never so much man as when he is striving for what is just beyond his grasp. Men go, always, to the mountains to find themselves.

I have no doubt whatsoever that Kent Evans went to the mountains for just these reasons, to test himself, to push his own fears and resources to the limits. To testify to this, let me read to you some paragraphs Kent wrote about his climbing experience a few weeks ago; as a final word, let Kent speak for himself:

"It was a rather easy Class Five route, but I was inexperienced and out of shape. As I snapped into my rope, my partner and I went through the ritual:

'Belay on,' she said. 'Climbing,' I replied. Yet I wouldn't have any protection until I put a 'biner into a bolt some fifteen feet above.

Nervously I climbed to a 'good ledge and, after some stretching, put the rope and 'biner into the hanger on the bolt. From this point I took the harder of the two crack systems, laybacking and jamming up about ten feet. At that point, I reached an impasse and stood in a tiring foot jam for several minutes. Finally I spotted the solution about a foot to my left. After this crux move, I scrambled up the crack and chimnied to the top.

With a sigh of relief, I yelled 'off belay,' down to my belayer. The ecstasy of the finished pitch move more than compensated for the doubts during the crux moves. I was ready to rappel off and yell, 'Climbing once again.'"

Kent Evans lived his life as an adventure – full tilt, straight ahead, on the electric edge of challenge, large and small. The way in which he lived and the way in which he died were far beyond his years. His journey stands as an invisible memorial on which are these words,

This was no Child, this was a Man.

Dona Nobis Pacem – Give us peace, Amen

RECESSIONAL

IN MEMORIAM

The following three items were written by Lakeside students immediately after Kent's death and were published in the "Lakeside Tattler," the school newspaper, On June 8, 1972.

Paul Carlson, class of 1973, was Kent's earliest friend at Lakeside. He writes with striking clarity about that friendship.

Tim Thompson, Class of 1972, worked closely with Kent on school scheduling and wrote this poem very soon after learning of his friend's death.

The poem "To Kent" by Lincoln Ferris, Class of 1973, is a biting portrayal of the instant, dehydrated plastic culture in which we, especially those of us who are young, live. It is a commentary on this culture written in the midst of distress. Note particularly the closing lines.

KENT EVANS by Paul Carlson

Kent and I met for the first time when we both came to Lakeside as seventh graders. Neither of us fit readily into any of the groups which quickly formed. We were both shy but became friends. We had interests and classes in common. We were both interested in politics of any kind. During eighth grade I withdrew from the race for Secretary-Treasurer and endorsed Kent; he lost anyway but we were both elected to the Lower School Senate. We were on free study together. Those things seem trivial now, but they meant something to us then.

That was 1968, the first election year we really remembered. We shared a few meaningful silly things: in French we marked our answers 'HHH' for right, 'RMN' for half–right, and 'GCW' for wrong; I was happy when I shook hands with Humphrey, but Kent evened the score by meeting Muskie. We campaigned for Humphrey, but Kent was more active than I. He went from headquarters to headquarters on Union Street, working for Humphrey, Magnuson and O'Connell. We went to other campaign headquarters – Nixon's, Wallace's, Metcalf's – to collect buttons and literature. Together we denounced Wallace and anti-fluoridation literature. We shared defeat and small triumphs the day after the election: Humphrey lost but carried Washington, and Magnuson was re–elected.

We were joyful when, at his house, we saw on TV that Kennedy had been elected Senate Whip. He liked the Kennedys more than I, but we were both pleased at Kennedy's victory and angry at Eugene McCarthy, who had voted against him.

We were miserable and happy together on the eighth grade hike, when our tents were pitched where the tide came in. We shared the companionship and comfort that followed, when we went to his house and shared the experience with his parents.

I went sailing with him once. Out on the Sound he was capable were I was clumsy, but nothing else changed. Being on the water added a new dimension to my life, and it did the same for him.

We talked on the phone for hours at a time. We said everything and nothing in a wild rambling that occasionally just reaffirmed our friendship without communicating much else.

In the summer of 1969 we went to Washington, D.C., for two weeks. We stayed at his cousin's apartment and wandered around the city. We went to the congressional galleries and felt admiration for Albert Gore and Shirley Chisholm, sadness and pity for Wright Patman, and dislike for George Murphy and Tom Pelly. We went on the Congressional Tour of the White House and laughed at ourselves when we found out how false our inflated notions of the tour were. We wandered through cavernous government buildings, picking up folders and pamphlets right and left. We experienced small triumphs on seeing Rogers and Romney testifying before Congressional committees. Above all, we explored everywhere, the places which tourists rarely see.

We lost something with Chappaquidick; our dreams, born with McCarthy in New Hampshire, died a little there. In politics, I suppose, we were pragmatic; we went for Humphrey without a qualm. But our loyalties were as fierce as the loyalties of idealists. Chappaquidick changed that. It demonstrated to us the fallibility of our heroes.

Our interests diverged, but we were always friends after that. We went to the University of Washington together on Earth Day. We saw films and picked up literature from the environmental groups, the Socialists and the Communists. The day was not entirely successful for us, but we enjoyed being together.

Occasionally we talked as deeply as before. At the beginning of this year we talked about politics. I intended to work for Muskie, and Kent thought he would too. But I didn't, and later found myself working for McGovern. When I discussed it with Kent, he was, as always, interested in what I had to say.

He was busy, as always. Possibly more than any other person in the class, he went out and did things, whether with politics, computers, or something else. His achievements were far greater than those of most of us his age.

He was also a very nice person. I'm glad I had a chance to know him well. I am grateful that I'll be able to remember his as he was in Washington, D.C. – friendly, cheerful, good natured, curious and interested in everything. That's the way to remember him.

My friend,

I weep with sadness so deep for your death;
And yet,
I weep with tears of joy for your life.
So clear to me still are the endless nights
of self-inflicted scheduling and lousy jokes,
and walking home at dawn in the rain.
So clear to me still is your voice announcing in distress
That the only kid who had no English class
Was named, alas, Lisa Ayrault.
So clear to me still is your Final Judgment
Pronounced against my Viennese-roast coffee,
In favor of Bayley's nefarious brew.
So clear to me still are the times without sleep,
When near the dawn, we no longer had to have fun
To enjoy ourselves and life.
My friend,
I weep with sadness so deep for your death;
And yet,
I weep with tears of joy for your life.
— Timothy Thompson

TO KENT
You were there
in my breakfast
digest.
Prepared
as all the rest
Set out on the oaken table
for me,
by me.
Processed like the Cheerios,
the bread:
milled and formed,
the sugar:
cut and refined,
the orange juice:
squeezed and rehydrated
You were there
with the pointing man.
The one they froze
and flattened,
transfixed on newsprint.
They condensed you,
tagged you.
into one short column.
But, I am one of them
and no better.
I took you from my doorstep,
laid you upon my table
and devoured you unashamed.
I have eaten you,
and now leave you
in lines upon a paper.
Less than I would
a piece of toast.
You are more.
More in memory
than just this.
I am sorry.
Death should not be had
in a breakfast digest.

EDITOR'S NOTE

As a newcomer in Marvin Evans' life, I don't know him nearly as well as his many lifelong friends. My impressions have grown from this memoir and as we talked about the memoir and other events in our lives.

Marvin always welcomes me at the door with a twinkle in his eyes as I'm sure he does with everyone. He is a man who on the whole has enjoyed his 84 years. His *joie de vivre* surely arises from his family life and the fact that so many doors have serendipitously opened along the way. The meeting, marriage, and equal relationship of Marvin and Mary certainly qualifies as such a gift. Nevertheless, the family faced and also weathered near tragedy and the finality of loss.

The solace from Marvin's lifelong love of the great Eastern Shore and Northwest bodies of water and memories of so many summers of smooth sailing speak for themselves. Having grown up in Baltimore, I've been pleasantly reminded of my younger years when we went boating and swimming in Chesapeake Bay. My current life on Puget Sound seems like a reunion.

Several times as we worked together, Marvin said he could write a whole book about his life as a Unitarian Minister and other periods of his life. Perhaps he will. For now, he wants to share these memories with good friends and offer testimonials to his wife and two sons. Kent's untimely death and his early promise, leaves a bittersweet taste of what might have been. David, his life all the more precious following Kent's death and his own close call, has now embraced life with his own family, his love of sailing, and other interests. I believe it is Marvin's intention to bequeath both family history and perspective to David. Even now, after years of caring for his beloved Mary as her health declined and slowing down, Marvin steadily stays the course.

Kathryn Keve

ACKNOWLEDGMENTS

Writing "Pearl's Boy" has been a deeply personal effort. Research meant pouring over the remains of an extensive collection of family archives assembled by my late wife, Mary Hood Evans.

I was helped by a host of friends who offered recollections, memories and unfailing encouragement. I'm especially grateful to David Evans and Alexis Johanson. Long conversations with them refreshed my knowledge and sharpened my perceptions.

The wisest thing I did, by far, was that at the outset, when only a few pages had been written, was to engage the professional services of Kathryn Keve. Working with her is an absolute delight because of her skills and also because of her keen understanding of the story and its author. It is acccurate to note that without her wise counsel, professional skills and personal insights, "Pearl's Boy" would never have gone to the printer.

Finally, an uncountable number of good friends, co-activists, co-workers and congregations have shared my life story. This journey has been taken in good company, and other than the early influence of Miss Pearl, this is what enables me to Say "Yes" to Life.

Marvin D. Evans
Bainbridge Island, WA
May 12, 2010